RiverFeast

Still Celebrating Cincinnati

Presented by
The Junior League of Cincinnati

The Junior League of Cincinnati is an exclusively educational and charitable organization. Its purpose is to improve the quality of life in Greater Cincinnati by developing trained volunteers, responsive to community needs.

All profits realized from the sale of this book are returned to the community through projects sponsored by the Junior League of Cincinnati.

Introduction

Cincinnati loves to celebrate. We'll find any excuse to do it. In the fall, it's tailgate parties at the Bengals games, mystical masquerades at Halloween, and election day parties. In the spring, we love to party on baseball's opening day, Derby Day, and April Fool's Day. Winter brings a host of great reasons to celebrate, from the twelve days of Christmas to Valentine's Day. In the summer of 1988, Cincinnati celebrated its Bicentennial. What a bash! The river was full of riverboats, including our own Delta Queen, decked out in their finest to celebrate the grand role of the Ohio River in Cincinnati's history. Thousands thronged on the shores of the river to take part in the city's biggest birthday party.

The Junior League of Cincinnati's first cookbook, **Cincinnati Celebrates**, paid tribute to the city's festive spirit. Now we are proud to present **RiverFeast: Still Celebrating Cincinnati**, a collection of recipes gathered from members, family and friends of the Junior League, in an effort to give back to this wonderful city in some small measure the joys of 200 years of exciting growth and change. This is our way of saying that we continually celebrate the energy, diversity, and joie de vivre of the people of our city. The proceeds from **RiverFeast** go into Junior League funded projects in Cincinnati, such as McKinley Flight School where Families Learning Is our Greatest Hope for Tomorrow, Pro Kids, Woman to Woman, Fernside: A Center for Grieving Children, and many others.

In this cookbook you will find over 350 recipes, all of which have been triple-tested. We owe many thanks to the volunteers, too numerous to list here, who have contributed their time and their palates for these all-important tests. These recipes were chosen for their emphasis on the use of fresh ingredients and their ease of preparation. We have also included a special selection of recipes from some of the city's long established and most prestigious restaurants, including our 5-star Maisonette. We hope you will enjoy them as much as we do!

RiverFeast Committee

1991 - 1992

Chair	Sue Saffin	
Co-chair	Karen Hock	
Marketing Chair	Wendy Wilson	
Treasurer	Karen Bidlingmeyer	
Marketing & Sales		
Holly Budig	Anne Davies	Lindsay Rorick
Beth Cork	Nancy Duran	Ann Thelen

1990 - 1991

Chair	Susan Chagares	
Co-chair	Sue Saffin	
Marketing Chair	Jeanne Morrison	
Treasurer	Karen Bidlingmeyer	
Sustaining Advisor	Cathy Kearns	
Marketing & Sales		
Sandy Bell	Mer Hauser	Lindsay Rorick
Dori Cambruzzi	Vada Kinnebrew	Ann Thelen
Anne Davies	Ann Leichty	Cathy Thomas
Nancy Duran	Sheila Miller	Candace Thurner
Carol Eastes	Chan Milton	Wendy Wilson
Lynn Grace	Helen Patch	

1990 - 1991

Chair	Cathy Kearns
Co-chair	Bobbi McCaslin
Board Liaisons	Ellie Berghausen
	Darlene Kamine
Communications	Jane Clarke
Editor	Emily Werrell
Marketing	Jeanne Morrison
& Sales	Susan Chagares
	Dionn Tron
Recipes	Susan Kahn
& Testing	Helen Patch
Treasurers	Carrie Hayden
	Karen Bidlingmeyer

Editor's Note

Desktop publishing is an extremely exciting option for non-profit groups such as the Junior League. When the JLC voted to produce a new cookbook as a fundraiser, it became clear that our new desktop publishing capabilities could be utilized. The computer committee and the cookbook committee began brainstorming and developed plans to design and produce the camera-ready artwork for **RiverFeast** ourselves, thus saving enormous sums earmarked for typists, typesetting and paste-up.

Enter Apple Computer, Inc., which offered its local training facility for our one-time use. An "Apple Core" of fifteen enthusiastic volunteers, headed by Carol Brouwer, Jan Kiefhaber and Emily Werrell, **RiverFeast** editor, pecked furiously away at the Macintosh computers in an extravaganza of recipe-entering.

The Junior League is, as always, very grateful to businesses in our city such as Apple Computer who support our volunteer efforts. Without corporate support, we would not be able to contribute so generously to our community.

The following volunteers enthusiastically contributed the hundreds of hours needed to complete **RiverFeast**.

Graphic Design	**Data Entry**
Jan Kiefhaber	Nancy Berg
Denise Strasser	Jane Clarke
Editing	Mary Beth Cornelius
Carol Brouwer	Linda DeLuca
Jan Kiefhaber	Patti English
Denise Strasser	Carrie Hayden
Truett Vondrak	Vicki Lauck
Emily Werrell	Mary LeRoy
Proofreading	Mary Lee Olinger
Carol Brouwer	Laura Pease
Cathy Kearns	Elyce Turba
Helen Patch	Debby Welsh
Emily Werrell	
Jane Woolsey	

Special thanks to Julie Mathews of Apple Computer.

RiverFeast Contributors

Lee Adams
Betsy Allyn
Linda Appleby
Nancy Aronson
Darci Beattie
Gaie Benecchi
Nancy Berg
Diana Berghausen
Ellie Berghausen
Carol Jolliffe Berutti
Jane Bidlingmeyer
Annette Bloomstrom
Deborah Blum
Ruth Anne Bohon
Janet Bornancin
Julia Boysen
Hazeleen Brewster
Mary Brinkmeyer
Cathy Burton
Jayne Byrnes
Barbara Cagle
Mary Ellen Carmichael
Anne Castleberry-Pund
Lucy Chagares
Susan Chagares
Judy Chandler
Jane Clarke
Nancy Creaghead
Lee Crooks
Ann Crossen
Carol Davidson
Leslie DeCourcy
Linda DeLuca
Billie DeMuth
Dianna Pund Doll
Florence Dowdy
Carol Eastes
Tara Eaton
Palmer Ellsworth
Judith Evans
Barbara Eveland
Sally Eversole
Nancy Fehr

Karen Fischer
Margaret Fisk
Barbara Fitch
Betsy Gallagher
Robin Galvin
Naomi Gardner
Delle Gay
Vallie Geier
Laura Getz
Sara Gilmore
Cindy Gore
Peggy Grosser
Clairanne Hann
Judy Hauser
Sharon Haydock
Marjorie Hiatt
Charlotte Hogue
Joyce Jackson
Lynn Jacobs
Anna Jefferson
Susan Johnson
Susan Kahn
Cathy Kearns
Alice Kelly
Anne Kelly
Barbara Korstanje
June Kottmeier
Jan Kramig
Pat Kropp
Margie Kyte
Cindi Lacy
Jill Lambert
Peggy Landes
Susan Laubenthal
M. Drue Lehmann
Ruthi Levering
Linda Lichtendahl
Gillian Littlehale
Deborah Loflin
Ruth Longenecker
Molly Lucien
Alice Lytle
Kristine Malkoski

Mary March
Kathy Marshall
Bobbi McCaslin
Frances McClure
Lois McConnell
Jeanne Morrison
Ginny Myer
Mary Lee Olinger
Geraldine Olson
Helen Patch
Sylvia Paxton
Laura Pease
Diane Peterson
Carol Philpott
Rebecca Podore
Jacqueline Reik
Marianne Rowe
Christine Schnurr
Nat Schoeny
Bobbee Schott
Martha Seaman
Linda Shad
Alane Shoemaker
Blair Smith
Linda Smith
Pamela Smith
Chris Stubbins
Eileen Stuhlreyer
Leslie Sukys
Kathleen Tenebaum
Dionn Tron
Elyce Turba
Maria Vincent
Margy Wachs
Rosemary Welsh
Eloise Werrell
Emily Werrell
William Werrell
Susan Westerling
Connie Williams
Janie Williams
Jo Ann Withrow
Marjorie Zbaren

Table of Contents

About the Artist

Thomas R. Greene, Jr. is a freelance illustrator/designer who has worked in the Cincinnati area for a number of years, producing art work for ad agencies, art studios, private firms and publishing companies across the country.

It's not surprising that Tom seems at home portraying the subject of steamboats since his grandparents, Mary and Gordon Greene, began the riverboat line, Greene Line Steamers, Inc. in 1890. Names of such boats as the Greenland, Chris Greene, Tom Greene (named after Tom's father), Gordon C. Greene and more recently, the Delta Queen, are well known to Cincinnatians and river-history enthusiasts.

Tom currently lives with his wife, Shirley, in a restored 150 year old farmhouse near Cedar Grove, Indiana. His art studio is a converted root-cellar/summer kitchen on the property. Tom attends to most of his freelance work there, but also lends his talents to the art department of a software marketing firm in Cincinnati.

Beverages
and
Appetizers

Ann's Spiced Nuts

1   egg white
1   teaspoon water
2   cups pecans or walnuts
$^1/_2$ cup sugar
$^1/_4$ teaspoon nutmeg
$^3/_4$ teaspoon salt
1   teaspoon cinnamon
Pinch ground cloves

Easy

Yield: 2 cups
May prepare ahead
Preparation time:
  10 minutes
Bake 30 minutes

Freezes well

Makes a great
Christmas gift!

Beat egg white with water until foamy. Stir nuts into egg white mixture, let stand for a few minutes. Mix together sugar and spices; add to nuts and stir well. Place onto a shallow buttered pan. Bake for 30 minutes at 300°, stirring often.

Armenian Meatballs

Easy

Yield: 18 meatballs
Preparation time:
 20 minutes
Bake 30 minutes

1   lb. ground lamb
1   cup shredded cheddar cheese
1   cup soft bread cubes
1   cup chopped parsley
$\frac{1}{3}$ cup chopped onions
$\frac{1}{2}$ tsp. salt
$\frac{1}{4}$ tsp. garlic salt
$\frac{1}{8}$ tsp. pepper
1   egg, slightly beaten
2   Tbsp. butter
1   8 oz. can tomato sauce
$\frac{1}{4}$ cup Parmesan cheese

Combine lamb, cheese, bread cubes, parsley, onion, salt, garlic salt, pepper and egg. Shape into 18 balls. Melt butter; brown meatballs over low heat. Remove to casserole and pour tomato sauce over meatballs. Sprinkle Parmesan on top. Cover; bake at 350° for 20 minutes. Remove cover, bake 10 minutes longer.

Baked Brie With Chutney

1   sheet frozen puff pastry

Prepared chutney to taste

1   whole, small, ripe wheel Brie cheese

1   egg, beaten

Thaw pastry according to package directions. Roll on floured surface until large enough to fully wrap Brie. Spread desired amount of chutney on top of cheese. Wrap pastry around cheese, tucking edges underneath. Trim excess pastry. Brush with beaten egg. Bake at 425° on a buttered baking sheet for 25–30 minutes, until puffed.

Easy

Serves 6–8
Preparation time:
 15 minutes
Bake 30 minutes

Freezes well

For a fancy presentation, cut decorative shapes from excess pastry and decorate before baking.

Bill's Hummus

2 cups chick peas (garbanzo beans), cooked (may be canned)
$^2/_3$ cup tahini (sesame butter)
$^3/_4$ cup lemon juice
5 cloves garlic
1 tsp. salt
1 lb. pita bread, cut into wedges
2 Tbsp. olive oil (optional)

Purée all ingredients, except bread and olive oil, in food processor or blender until smooth. Pour into an attractive bowl (may be prepared ahead to this point and refrigerated). To serve, make a puddle of olive oil in the middle of the bowl of hummus (optional). Serve with wedges of pita bread.

Brown Sugar Bacon

2 lb. bacon (thickly sliced, best grade)
$^3/_4$ cup brown sugar

Lay bacon in foil-lined rectangular cake pans, with edges of bacon just touching. Sprinkle brown sugar over top. Bake at 250° for $1^1/_2$ hours. Pour off grease. Bake 30 minutes more. Remove from pan immediately; drain on waxed paper or brown paper. Store between sheets of waxed paper, in airtight container, in refrigerator.

Buffalo Chicken Wings

5   lb. (25–30) chicken wings
1    $2^1/_2$ oz. bottle hot pepper sauce (use more
     or less to taste)
1   cup butter, melted
1   Tbsp. seasoned salt

Dip:
1   cup mayonnaise
$^1/_2$ cup sour cream
2   oz. blue cheese
Dash onion powder
Dash garlic powder
1   Tbsp. lemon juice

Easy

Yield: 50-60
 appetizers
May prepare ahead
Preparation time:
 10 minutes
Marinate overnight
 or several hours
Bake 25 minutes

Freezes well

Split wings and discard tips. Spread on cookie sheet and bake 20 minutes at 400°. Combine hot pepper sauce, melted butter and salt. Marinate chicken in sauce for several hours or overnight (may be frozen at this point). Before serving, bake for 5 minutes on each side at 400°; turning to brown. Serve with blue cheese dip sprinkled with parsley.

Dip:
Combine mayonnaise and sour cream. Mash blue cheese into mixture with a fork. Add all other ingredients, mix well.

7

Caramel Corn

Easy

Yield: 6 quarts
Prepare ahead
Preparation time:
 10 minutes
Bake 1 hour

6   quarts popped corn (no salt or butter)
2   sticks (1 cup) butter or margarine
2   cups firmly packed brown sugar
$\frac{1}{2}$ cup light corn syrup
1   tsp. salt
$\frac{1}{2}$ tsp. baking soda
1   tsp. vanilla

Put popcorn in a turkey roaster or large foil pan. Melt butter in medium saucepan over medium heat. Add brown sugar, corn syrup and salt and stir until it starts to boil. Boil 5 minutes without stirring. Stir in baking soda and vanilla and pour over popped corn. Put roaster uncovered into oven and bake for 1 hour at 250°, stirring every 15 minutes. Remove from oven, stirring to keep corn from sticking together, until cool. Store in airtight container.

Caviar Pie

4 hard boiled eggs, chopped
Mayonnaise
8 oz. sour cream
8 oz. cream cheese, softened
Grated onion
2 2 oz. jars caviar (red, black or golden)

Easy

Serves 6–8
May prepare ahead
Preparation time:
   20 minutes
Chill 1 hour

Mix the chopped egg with enough mayonnaise to bind together. (It should not be wet enough for sandwiches.) Spread into bottom of 9" pie or quiche pan. Chill until firm. Blend the sour cream and cream cheese together until smooth. (Do not use a food processor or you will end up with caviar soup.) Grate enough onion into the sour cream mixture that you can see onion pieces when you stir. Spread gently on top of chilled chopped egg. Chill until firm. Spread caviar evenly on top and serve with plain toast or crackers.

Hint: If inexpensive caviar is used, rinsing it first in a wire strainer and blotting the bottom of the strainer on paper towels helps keep the caviar juices from running all over the white layer of cream cheese and sour cream. Using two different caviars (red and black) looks very pretty. Use foil to cover half the dish while you spread the other half with one color, then carefully repeat the process.

Cheezy Chicken Wings

Easy

Serves 15–20
Preparation time:
 30 minutes
Bake 1 hour

2   cups grated Parmesan cheese
4   Tbsp. chopped parsley
2   tsp. oregano
4   tsp. paprika
1   tsp. red pepper
2   tsp. salt (optional)
2   sticks butter
3   lb. chicken wings

Mix together cheese, parsley, oregano, paprika, red pepper, and salt. Melt butter in saucepan. Roll chicken wings in butter, then in mixed ingredients. Place wings on foil-lined baking sheet with lip. Bake $1/2$ hour at 350°, drain grease. Bake another $1/2$ hour and serve immediately.

Cherokee
Cheese-O-Ritos

1 lb. refried beans
$1/_2$ tsp. ground cumin
$1/_4$ tsp. garlic powder
1 cup shredded Monterey Jack cheese
$1 1/_2$ lb. ground beef
3 6-oz. cans green chili salsa
6 flour tortillas (10-inch)
$3/_4$ lb. shredded colby cheese
2 large fresh tomatoes, peeled and diced
Sliced green onions and tops
Shredded lettuce
Sour cream (optional)

Moderate

Serves 6
*Partially prepare
  ahead*
*Preparation time:
  30 minutes*
Bake 30 minutes

Combine beans, cumin, garlic powder and Monterey Jack cheese in the top of a double boiler. Cook over hot water, covered, until cheese melts, stirring occasionally. Keep mixture hot until ready to use. Crumble beef into heated skillet. Cook over moderate heat, stirring frequently, until browned. Drain grease. Add 2 cans chili salsa; bring to a boil. Reduce heat and simmer, uncovered, until most of the liquid evaporates. Spread bean mixture on tortillas. Spread meat over beans, firmly pressing it into them. Lightly roll tortillas. Place them, seam side down, in a single layer in a well-greased, shallow 9x13 inch dish. Pour the third can of salsa over top and around sides of dish. Sprinkle colby cheese, tomatoes and onions on top. Bake, uncovered, at 350° for 30 minutes. Serve on plate surrounded with shredded lettuce, additional heated salsa and/or sour cream on the side.

Chutney Cheese Ball

Easy

*Yield: 2 large or 4
  small balls*
May prepare ahead
*Preparation time:
  15 minutes*

Freezes well

2   8 oz. pkg. cream cheese
$\frac{1}{2}$ cup spicy chutney, chopped
3–4 tsp. curry powder
$\frac{1}{2}$ tsp. dry mustard
Chopped pecans

Mix first 4 ingredients and refrigerate. When chilled, form into balls. Roll in nuts.

Classy Classic Artichoke Casserole

Moderate

Serves 8
May prepare ahead
*Preparation time:
  30 minutes*
Bake 40 minutes

Freezes well

2   14 oz. cans artichoke hearts
1   cup mayonnaise
1   cup Parmesan and Romano grated cheese
Dash Tabasco sauce
Dash garlic salt (optional)
$\frac{1}{2}$ tsp. fresh lemon juice
1   pkg. phyllo dough sheets
1   stick melted butter

Place artichoke hearts, mayonnaise and cheese in food processor and mix well (can be done by hand, leaving larger pieces, if desired). Add Tabasco, garlic salt and lemon juice. Grease an 8" or 9" glass pie plate; place one phyllo sheet across bottom, leaving edges extended. Add 5 or 6 additional phyllo sheets, buttering between each one with melted butter on a pastry brush. Place artichoke mixture in center of pie plate. Fold over each extended sheet (don't worry about appearance), buttering each layer. Place 2–4 new phyllo sheets over the "ball," remembering to butter each one. Trim at base. Bake for 40 minutes at 350°.

Crab Meltaways

1	5 oz. jar Old English cheese
1	stick butter
1	6–7 oz. can crabmeat
$^1/_2$	tsp. garlic salt
Pinch seasoned salt	
1	tsp. mayonnaise
6	split English muffins

Easy

Serves 16
Partially prepare
* ahead*
Preparation time:
* 20 minutes*
Freeze 30 minutes
Broil 5 minutes

Freezes well

Mix first six ingredients with mixer until well blended. Spread on one side of each of 12 muffin halves. Freeze at least $^1/_2$ hour (can be frozen several weeks). Thaw slightly and slice each muffin into quarters. Broil while still partially frozen until golden brown. Serve warm.

Curried Cheese Pâté

Easy

Serves 12–16
May prepare ahead
Preparation time:
 20 minutes
Chill at least 4 hours

Freezes well

*Adapt this recipe to
the seasons: shape
like a Christmas
tree, or garnish with
kumquat leaves at
Thanksgiving, or
marigolds in the
summer.*

2   8 oz. pkg. cream cheese
2   cups grated sharp cheddar cheese
6   Tbsp. sherry
2   Tbsp. Worcestershire sauce
2–3 tsp. curry powder
½   tsp. salt

Topping:
1   8 oz. jar chutney
½-¾ cup peanuts
½   cup chopped green onions
½   cup grated coconut

Cream cheeses together with sherry, Worcestershire sauce, curry and salt (can be done in food processor). Line 8" cake pan with plastic wrap, fill with cheese mixture. Cover top with plastic wrap and chill at least 4 hours. (Can be frozen at this point; defrost at room temperature.) Unmold cheese pâté on large platter. Garnish with layers of chutney, peanuts, green onions, and coconut. Serve with plain crackers.

Curried Crudité Dip

1 cup mayonnaise
4 tsp. soy sauce
2 tsp. dried onion flakes
1 tsp. curry powder
$\frac{1}{2}$ tsp. Beau Monde
2 tsp. milk
2 tsp. white vinegar
1 tsp. ginger

Easy

Yield: 1 cup
May prepare ahead
Preparation time:
*   10 minutes*
Chill 1 hour

Mix all ingredients together. Cover and refrigerate at least one hour before serving. Serve with raw vegetables.

Curry Cheddar Cheese Puffs

1 cup grated cheddar cheese
$\frac{1}{3}$ cup chopped green onion
$\frac{1}{3}$ cup pitted black olives
1 cup mayonnaise
1 Tbsp. curry powder
1 French baguette, thinly sliced

Easy

Serves 10
Partially prepare
* ahead*
Preparation time:
* 15 minutes*
Broil 5–10 minutes

Mix together cheese, green onion, olives, mayonnaise and curry powder (may be prepared ahead on same day). Heap onto bread slices. Broil 5–10 minutes, until cheese mixture puffs up.

Cherry Tomatoes
Stuffed with Blue Cheese

Easy

Serves 10–12
May prepare ahead
Preparation time:
* 30–40 minutes*

This is an attractive dish and looks festive at Christmas time.

30–36 cherry tomatoes
Salt
³/₄   cup small curd cottage cheese
¹/₂   cup crumbled blue cheese
2   Tbsp. finely chopped onion
Pepper
¹/₄   cup sour cream
Dill

Cut a thin slice from the top of each tomato. With a small melon ball cutter, scoop out pulp. Sprinkle shells with salt, invert them on a rack and let them drain for 15 minutes. In a bowl combine the cottage cheese, blue cheese, onion and salt and pepper to taste. Bind the mixture with sour cream. Fill the tomatoes with the mixture and sprinkle with dill.   For an especially attractive effect, pipe filling into tomatoes or reserve "caps" and place back on top of tomatoes after they are filled.

Dates, Hot Dates

Easy

Serves 6
Partially prepare
  ahead
Preparation time:
  20–30 minutes
Bake 15–20 minutes

$^1/_2$ lb. bacon
1   6 oz. tin salted, roasted almonds
1   8 oz. package pitted dates

Cut each strip of bacon into 3 pieces of equal length. Insert an almond into each date where the pit used to be. Wrap each date with a piece of bacon; secure with a toothpick. Arrange on a cookie sheet; bake at 400° for 15–20 minutes or until bacon is crisp.

Dill Dip

Easy

Yield: 2¹/₂ cups
May prepare ahead
Preparation time:
 10 minutes
Chill overnight

For an attractive presentation, serve in a hollowed-out red cabbage and garnish with fresh dill.

1¹/₃ cups lean sour cream or yogurt
1¹/₃ cups lowfat mayonnaise
2   Tbsp. dried parsley flakes
2   Tbsp. dried dill weed
2   tsp. seasoned salt
3–4 drops Tabasco sauce
2   tsp. Worcestershire sauce
1   pkg. green onion dip mix

Mix all ingredients together well. Chill overnight. Serve with raw vegetables.

Dutch Dip

Moderate

Serves 12
Prepare ahead
Preparation time:
 25 minutes
Chill 30 minutes

For more spice, add a dash of cayenne or curry to the cottage cheese. To vary, add slivered almonds or bacon bits

1   whole Dutch Edam cheese
2   lb. small curd cottage cheese
¹/₄ cup sour cream
6   Tbsp. chopped parsley or chives
2   tsp. horseradish sauce, or more to taste
Salt
Paprika
Crackers and/or raw vegetable sticks

Cut a slice from the top of the cheese and cut the edge in a zig-zag pattern using a sharp knife. With a melon ball cutter, scoop out as many balls of cheese as possible. Using a spoon, hollow out remaining cheese, leaving empty shell. (Reserve odd bits of cheese for some other use.) Place cottage cheese in a bowl and beat with a wooden spoon to soften it. Mix in the sour cream, parsley and horseradish. Season well with salt and paprika. Stand the Edam shell on a large platter and pile in the cottage cheese mixture. Chill about 30 minutes. Serve surrounded with scooped-out cheese balls, crackers and raw vegetables.

Fast and Delicious
Shrimp Dip

1	8 oz. pkg. cream cheese
¹/₂	cup mayonnaise
1	Tbsp. minced or grated onion
1	Tbsp. lemon juice
10	drops Tabasco sauce
1 or 2	4 oz. cans tiny shrimp, rinsed

Easy

Serves 10
May prepare ahead
Preparation time:
10 –15 minutes
Chill 1 hour

Cream together first five ingredients. Fold in the tiny shrimp. Let stand in refrigerator at least 1 hour. Serve with fresh vegetables or crackers.

Fiesta Dip

1 16 oz. can refried beans
$^1/_2$ tsp. chili powder
2 avocados
$^1/_2$ cup mayonnaise
4 pieces cooled bacon, crumbled
$^1/_2$ cup chopped onion
1 cup chopped black olives
1 cup chopped tomatoes
1 4 oz. can green chilies, chopped
1 cup shredded Monterey Jack or cheddar
   cheese

Combine beans and chili powder; mix well. Combine avocados, mayonnaise, bacon and onion; mix well. Layer in a 10"–12" deep dish pie plate, starting with beans, then adding avocado mixture, olives, tomatoes, chilies, and topping with cheese. Serve with large round tostado chips.

French Brie Brillant

$^1/_2$ lb. French Brie cheese
$^1/_4$ cup sour cream
10 black olives, minced
1 Tbsp. chopped onions
Toast points

Have cheese at room temperature. Blend with sour cream. Add olives and onions. Chill until ready to serve. Remove one hour before serving. Spread on toast points and broil 2–3 minutes until cheese is bubbly. Serve hot.

Garlic Almonds

1   Tbsp. butter
2   Tbsp. soy sauce
3   tsp. Tabasco sauce
3   tsp. garlic powder
1   lb. whole blanched almonds
3   tsp. lemon pepper
$^1/_2$ tsp. dried red pepper flakes

Easy

Yield: 1 pound
May prepare ahead
Preparation time:
 10 minutes
Bake 20 minutes

Preheat oven to 250°. Coat baking sheet with butter. Mix soy sauce, Tabasco and garlic powder together in bowl. Spread almonds on cookie sheet, then pour over mixture, stirring to coat well. Sprinkle on $1^1/_2$ tsp. lemon pepper and bake 10 minutes. Stir well, add remaining pepper and flakes. Bake 10 minutes more. Cool. Store overnight in airtight container.

Guacamole

Easy

Serves 10–12
Preparation time:
 15 minutes

Perfect with margaritas.

$^1/_2$ cup finely chopped onion
1   medium tomato
1   small dried red pepper
6   peeled, ripe avocados
2   tsp. salt
2   Tbsp. lemon juice
1   Tbsp. mayonnaise
1   tsp. Crisco® oil
6   drops Tabasco sauce

Chop together, in food processor or by hand, the onion, tomato, and dried red pepper. Chop avocadoes into small chunks (do not mash). Add onion mixture and remaining ingredients to avocados, mix by hand. Serve with tortilla chips.

Hanky Pankys

Easy

Serves 50
May prepare ahead
Preparation time:
30 minutes
Bake 20 minutes

Freezes well

1   lb. ground beef
1   lb. bulk hot sausage
1   tsp. oregano
1   tsp. Worcestershire sauce
$^1/_2$ tsp. black pepper
$^1/_2$ tsp. garlic salt
1   lb. Velveeta cheese, cut in chunks
$1^1/_2$ loaves miniature ("party") rye bread

Brown ground beef and sausage; drain. Combine all remaining ingredients; add to beef mixture. Heat until cheese melts. Spread on bread slices. Freeze on cookie sheets; store in plastic bags until needed. Bake at 350° for 20 minutes.

Hot Crabmeat Dip

¼ cup butter
10 oz. sharp cheddar cheese,
    cut into small pieces
8   oz. sharp American cheese,
    cut into small pieces
½ cup sauterne wine
6–8 oz. fresh or frozen crabmeat, flaked

Easy

Serves 20
Preparation time:
  15 minutes
Cook 10 minutes

Melt butter and cheeses over low heat. Add sauterne, stirring to mix well. Add crabmeat, pour into chafing dish. Serve with crackers.

Hot Spinach Balls

Easy

*Yield: about 100
  small appetizers*
May prepare ahead
*Preparation time:
  35 minutes*
Bake 20 minutes

Freezes well

4   large eggs
2   10 oz. boxes frozen spinach, cooked according to package instructions, drained and squeezed dry
1   cup grated onion
³/₄ cup melted butter
¹/₂ tsp. salt
¹/₂ tsp. thyme
¹/₂ tsp nutmeg
¹/₂ tsp. black pepper
2¹/₂ cups crumb-type herb stuffing mix

Beat eggs. Stir in remaining ingredients except stuffing mix. When well blended, stir in mix and allow to rest 20 minutes. Shape into small balls. Arrange on ungreased baking sheet; bake at 350° for 20 minutes. Balls may be cooled, wrapped and frozen. Reheat on baking sheet 10–15 minutes at 350°.

Make Ahead Meatballs

3 lb. ground beef
$^1/_2$ cup chopped onion
$^1/_2$ cup chopped celery
2 Tbsp. butter
1 large bottle catsup
1 tsp. chili powder
1 tsp. dry mustard
3 Tbsp. Worcestershire sauce
2 Tbsp. brown sugar
4 Tbsp. lemon juice
2 Tbsp. vinegar
1 cup water
Salt and pepper to taste

Easy

Yield: 60 small
meatballs
Prepare ahead
Preparation time:
30 minutes
Marinate 2–3 days

Freezes well

Form ground beef into small meatballs. Sauté onions and celery in butter. Add meatballs and brown. Mix all remaining ingredients in large dutch oven. Bring to a boil, then add meatballs and simmer for 30 minutes. Cool, cover and store in refrigerator for 2-4 days. Simmer 3–4 hours before serving in chafing dish.

Marinated Lemon Shrimp

Easy

Serves 12
May prepare ahead
Preparation time:
  20 minutes
Marinate overnight

Serve on a bed of lettuce for a pretty salad.

3 lb. cooked shrimp
2 cups small black olives
1¹/₂ cups lemon juice
6 Tbsp. wine vinegar
¹/₄ cup olive oil
2 thinly sliced lemons
2 thinly sliced purple onions
5 cloves garlic
2 Tbsp. dry mustard
¹/₄ tsp. pepper
1 Tbsp. salt
¹/₂ tsp. turmeric

Toss all ingredients together in a large bowl. Marinate overnight. Serve with toothpicks.

Marinated Mushrooms

Easy

Serves 8
Prepare ahead
Preparation time:
  15 minutes
Marinate overnight

This will keep in the refrigerator for several days

1¹/₂ lb. fresh mushrooms, caps only
¹/₄ cup Crisco® oil
¹/₂ cup vinegar
2 Tbsp. sugar
1 medium onion, chopped
¹/₄ cup ketchup
1 tsp. seasoned salt
1 tsp. pepper
¹/₄ tsp. thyme
1 bay leaf
¹/₄ tsp. garlic powder

Simmer mushrooms in boiling, salted water for 2–3 minutes, drain and set aside. Combine remaining ingredients. Add mushrooms, refrigerate overnight.

Nancy's Antipasto

1	cup olive oil
¹/₂	cup vinegar
1	14-oz. bottle ketchup
1	Tbsp. salt
2	Tbsp. capers
5	sweet pickles, chopped
3	13-oz. cans white tuna
¹/₂	tube anchovy paste
2	4-oz. jars mushroom caps
1	8-oz. jar cocktail onions
1	3-oz. jar stuffed green olives, sliced
1	cup chopped celery
1	cup chopped raw cauliflower

Easy

Serves 20–30
May prepare ahead
Preparation time:
  20 minutes
Chill 2 hours

Serves a crowd!

Combine all ingredients; chill 2 hours. Serve with crisp crackers.

Mushroom Croustades

Moderate

Yield: 24 crous-
  tades
Partially prepare
  ahead
Preparation time:
  1 hour
Cook 20 minutes

Perfect for an hors
d' oeuvres buffet

24   slices white bread
2   Tbsp. very soft butter

Filling:
4   Tbsp. butter
3   Tbsp. finely chopped shallots
$\frac{1}{2}$ lb. mushrooms, chopped fine
2   level Tbsp. flour
1   cup heavy cream
$\frac{1}{2}$ tsp. salt
$\frac{1}{8}$ tsp. cayenne pepper
1   Tbsp. finely chopped parsley
$1\frac{1}{2}$ Tbsp. finely chopped chives
$\frac{1}{2}$ tsp. lemon juice
2   Tbsp. Parmesan cheese

For 24 croustades, use a 3" round cutter and cut a round from each slice of bread. Coat inside of each 2" wide muffin tins (12 to a tin) with butter. Push the rounds into the tins, molding them to form a perfect cup. Bake in preheated 400° oven for 10 minutes or until brown. Remove and cool.

Filling:
Melt butter in heavy 10" skillet. Add shallots and stir constantly over moderate heat for about 4 minutes. Do not brown. Stir in mushrooms; coat thoroughly with butter and let cook without stirring. In a few minutes they will give off a good deal of liquid. Stir them

now occasionally and continue to cook until all moisture has evaporated (10–15 minutes). Remove from heat and sprinkle flour over mixture; stir thoroughly. Pour cream over mixture, stirring constantly. Bring to a boil; lower heat to the barest simmer and cook a minute or two longer to remove any taste of raw flour. Remove from heat and add salt, cayenne, parsley, chives and lemon juice. Transfer to bowl and cool, covered, in refrigerator until ready to fill croustades. Fill croustades and bake at 350° for about 10 minutes. (Croustades can be stuffed and frozen if desired.) Sprinkle a dash of Parmesan on top of each croustade and serve.

Parmesan Pita Chips

6 rounds pita bread
$^3/_4$ cup melted butter
$1^1/_2$ cups grated Parmesan cheese

Cut pita pockets in half, then split in half. Brush with melted butter, sprinkle with cheese and cut each into 4 wedges. Place in single layer on baking sheet. Bake at 350° for 12–15 minutes.

Easy

Serves 16
Partially prepare ahead
Preparation time: 20 minutes
Bake 12–15 minutes

Good accompaniment to soups or dips

Pretty Hot Stuff

Easy

Serves 8–10
Preparation time:
15 minutes

1   lb. hot Italian sausage, casing removed
1   lb. Velveeta® cheese
1   10-ounce can Ro-Tel® tomatoes and green chilies

Brown sausage and set aside. Melt Velveeta® cheese in double boiler. Add sausage. Drain tomatoes and green chilies, reserving liquid. Add to cheese mixture. Mix thoroughly, adding some of the reserved liquid if desired. Serve in a chafing dish with tortilla chips.

Shrimp and Curry Dip

Easy

Serves 12
May prepare ahead
Preparation time:
20 minutes

1   8 oz. pkg. cream cheese, softened
$^1/_4$ cup sour cream
1   Tbsp. lemon juice
1   tsp. curry powder; more to taste
$^1/_4$ tsp. salt
1       $4^1/_4$ oz. can tiny cleaned shrimp, drained
1   hard-cooked egg, chopped
3   Tbsp. finely chopped green onions with tops
1   box wheat crackers

Blend cream cheese, sour cream, lemon juice, curry powder and salt. Spread about $^1/_4$" thick on an 8" plate. Top with shrimp, then egg; sprinkle with green onions. Serve with crackers.

Shrimp Butter

2   cups diced or mashed cooked shrimp
1   8 oz. pkg. softened cream cheese
1   stick butter
Juice of 1 lemon
1   small onion, finely chopped or grated
2   Tbsp. mayonnaise
Salt and pepper to taste

Blend all ingredients until smooth. Refrigerate until ready to serve. Serve with crackers.

Easy

Serves 10–12
May prepare ahead
Preparation time:
 15 minutes

Freezes well

This can be frozen or kept in refrigerator for several days.

Shrimp Cheese Dip

2   4$^1/_2$ oz. cans shrimp, deveined and mashed
8$^1/_2$ oz. sharp cheddar cheese, grated
2   small onions, grated
1$^1/_2$ cups mayonnaise (or to taste)
$^1/_8$ tsp. garlic salt
$^1/_8$ tsp. red pepper (or to taste)

Combine all ingredients. Chill and serve with crackers.

Easy

Serves 15–20
May prepare ahead
Preparation time:
 20 minutes

Snow Peas Stuffed with Shrimp

Moderate

Serves 6
May prepare ahead
Preparation time:
  1 hour
Marinate 1 hour

Sherry vinaigrette:
1   Tbsp. Dijon mustard
$^1/_4$ cup sherry vinegar
$^1/_2$ tsp. salt
Ground pepper to taste
2   minced garlic cloves
$1^1/_2$ cups olive oil

Snow peas:
2   Tbsp. peanut oil
1   lb. raw shrimp (about 18),
      peeled and deveined
1   cup sherry vinaigrette
18   snow peas (about $^1/_2$ lb.)
Salt to taste

Sherry vinaigrette:
Whisk mustard and sherry vinegar together in small bowl. Stir in salt, pepper and garlic. Whisking constantly, dribble oil into vinegar mixture in a slow, steady stream. Cover until ready to use.

Snow peas:
Heat half the peanut oil in small skillet. Sauté half the shrimp, stirring frequently for 4 minutes. Remove with slotted spoon, set aside. Repeat with remaining oil and shrimp. Pour $^1/_2$ cup sherry vinaigrette over warm shrimp. Let stand 1 hour. Trim snow peas and drop into kettle of boiling water. Cook 2 minutes. Drain

and plunge into ice water immediately. Cool peas and drain. Split them open along seams, leaving the halves joined at one end. Place one shrimp in each snow pea and skewer with toothpick. Arrange on platter, cover and chill until ready to serve. Drizzle remaining sherry vinaigrette over them before serving.

Stuffed Mushrooms

18   large mushrooms
18   slices bacon
³/₄   cup pecans
1   cup Italian-style bread crumbs
¹/₂   stick margarine
¹/₂   cup milk

Easy

Serves 8
May prepare ahead
Preparation time:
  20 minutes

Remove stems from mushrooms. Cook and crumble bacon. Chop pecans. Mix bacon, pecans, bread crumbs, margarine and milk. Fill caps and place on greased baking sheet. Bake at 350° for 15 minutes.

Tangy Crabmeat Dip

Easy

Serves 8
May prepare ahead
Preparation time:
* 10 minutes*
Refrigerate over-
* night*

6–8 oz. frozen or fresh crabmeat, drained
$^1/_2$ cup mayonnaise
1 clove garlic, minced
1 tsp. mustard
1 Tbsp. Worcestershire sauce
$^1/_8$ tsp. Tabasco sauce
$^1/_8$ tsp. salt
$^1/_2$ cup chili sauce
1 Tbsp. horseradish (or to taste)
2 hard cooked eggs, chopped

Drain and flake crabmeat. Combine all remaining ingredients; add crabmeat. Refrigerate overnight. Serve with salty crackers or chips.

Vegetable Pizza

Easy

Serves 15–20
Partially prepare
* ahead*
Preparation time:
* 30 minutes*
Cook 4–6 minutes

2 cans crescent dinner rolls
$^1/_2$ pkg. dry ranch dressing mix
$^3/_4$ cup mayonnaise
1 8 oz. pkg. cream cheese
$^1/_4$ cup shredded carrots
$^1/_4$ cup cauliflower flowerets
$^1/_4$ cup black olives
$^1/_4$ cup broccoli flowerets
$^1/_2$ cup shredded cheddar cheese
$^1/_2$ cup shredded mozzarella

Press rolls into jelly roll pan. Bake according to instructions and cool. Mix dressing mix, mayonnaise and cream cheese. Shred vegetables. Spread dressing mixture onto cooled crust. Sprinkle with vegetables and cheeses. Chill until ready to serve. Bake 4–6 minutes at 375°.

Water Chestnuggets

Easy

Serves 12
Partially prepare
  ahead
Preparation time:
  30 minutes
Broil 6 minutes

1   cup sugar
$^1/_2$ cup vinegar
$^1/_2$ cup water
$1^1/_2$ tsp. pepper
1   tsp. salt
2   Tbsp. cornstarch
2   Tbsp. water
$^3/_4$ tin dehydrated sweet pepper flakes
1   Tbsp. chili sauce
2   lb. bacon
2   cans whole water chestnuts

Combine first 5 ingredients in saucepan; boil 5 minutes. Make a paste of cornstarch and water; add to sauce, along with pepper flakes and chili sauce. Cut each bacon slice into three pieces. Drain water chestnuts and cut each in half. Wrap each water chestnut with bacon strip, secure with toothpick. Broil 3 minutes on each side. Serve in hot sauce in chafing dish.

Wild Rice Pea Pods

Easy

Serves 4–6
Partially prepare
ahead
Preparation time:
1 hour

1 lb. snow pea pods
4 cups cooked wild rice, chilled
$^1/_2$ cup golden raisins
$^1/_3$ cup chopped walnuts
$^1/_3$ cup mayonnaise
$^1/_3$ cup sour cream
$^1/_2$ tsp. curry powder
Salt to taste

Remove strings from pea pods and split open. Blanch 1 minute and rinse in cold water. Combine remaining ingredients. Fill pea pods with mixture and chill. Filling can be made 24 hours ahead; filled pea pods can be chilled 4–6 hours.

Zesty Cheese Crackers

Easy

Yield: 48 crackers
May prepare ahead
Preparation time:
10 minutes
Chill 2 hours
Bake 10 minutes

Ideal to have stored
in the freezer for last
minute guests.

8 oz. cheddar cheese, grated and softened
3 Tbsp. margarine or butter, softened
$^3/_4$ cup flour
$1^1/_2$ tsp. Worcestershire sauce
$^1/_2$ tsp. Tabasco sauce
$1^1/_4$ tsp. salt

Using food processor with dough blade, combine all ingredients. The mixture will look crumbly. Knead with hands and shape into a 12" long log. Wrap well and chill about 2 hours. When ready to use, slice into $\frac{1}{4}$" crackers. Bake on cookie sheet at 350° for 10 minutes or until very slightly golden around edges. Serve hot or at room temperature.

Zingy Gazpacho Mold

1   envelope unflavored gelatin
$1\frac{1}{4}$ cup stewed tomatoes, reserve liquid
$\frac{1}{2}$ cup Catalina® dressing
$\frac{1}{2}$ cup red or mild onion
$\frac{1}{4}$ cup green and red pepper
$\frac{1}{4}$ cup seedless chopped cucumber
Marinated broccoli (approximately 1 bunch)
Marinated cauliflower (approx 1 head), or 2
     cups cottage cheese

Easy

Serves 8
May prepare ahead
Preparation time:
1 hour

Add $\frac{1}{4}$ cup stewed tomatoes to envelope of gelatin. Stir over low heat until dissolved. Add 1 cup stewed tomatoes with liquid and Catalina® dressing. Mix well and chill until slightly thick. When thick, add onion, green and red pepper and cucumber. Chill in a 2 cup ring mold. Fill center with marinated cauliflower or cottage cheese. Spread broccoli around outside. Use red leaf lettuce as garnish.

Coffee Liquor

Easy

Yield: 1¹/₂ quarts
Prepare ahead
Preparation time:
20 minutes
Cook 30 minutes
Store 4 weeks

A delightful Christ-mas gift. Make the week before Thanksgiving for Christmas stocking stuffers.

3³/₄	cups sugar
1¹/₂"	vanilla bean, broken into pieces
2	cups water
3³/₄	Tbsp. instant coffee
¹/₄	cup boiling water
1	quart vodka

Combine sugar, vanilla pieces and water in a sauce pan. Cook on medium-low for 30 minutes without stirring. Mix coffee with boiling water; stir into above mixture. Strain, then stir in vodka. Place into small collector bottles, let cool, then cork tops. Store in a dark, cool place for 4 weeks.

Coffee Punch

Easy

Serves 10
Preparation time:
  15 minutes

A summer party punch

¹/₂	gallon coffee ice cream
1	large bottle (28 oz.) cream soda
1	large bottle (28 oz) ginger ale

Let ice cream soften a little in punch bowl before mixing ingredients. Slowly pour equal quantities of cream soda and ginger ale into punch bowl over ice cream. Mix slowly to prevent too much foam.

Nancy's Slush Punch

3	3 oz. boxes Jello® (select color)
7	cups boiling water
4	cups sugar
2	46 oz. cans pineapple juice
1	oz. almond extract
12	oz. lemon juice
6	cups water
2	quarts ginger ale

Easy

Yield: 50 cups
Prepare ahead
Preparation time:
* 20 minutes*

A good children's party punch.

Dissolve Jello® in 3 cups boiling water. Dissolve sugar in 4 remaining cups boiling water. Combine Jello® and sugar mixtures and add pineapple juice, almond extract and lemon juice. Add water; let mixture cool. Place in containers, leaving 1 inch room at top, and freeze. Remove from freezer at least three hours prior to serving. Break up mixture with ice pick or spoon. Place in punch bowl; add ginger ale.

Sparkling Pink Punch

Easy

Yield: 12 quarts
Preparation time:
30 minutes

1	cup red hots
1	cup sugar
2	cups water
4	46 oz. cans pineapple juice, chilled
4	quarts ginger ale, chilled
2	quarts club soda, chilled

Combine red hots, sugar and water and heat until completely dissolved, stirring constantly. Cool, add remaining ingredients. Serve immediately in a large punch bowl with ice ring, stirring frequently.

Soups
and
Salads

Broccoli Cream Soup

1 pkg. (10 oz.) frozen chopped broccoli
$1/_2$ cup frozen chopped onions
1 can ($10^3/_4$ oz.) condensed chicken broth
2 Tbsp. butter
2 Tbsp. flour
2 cups half and half
1 tsp. salt
$1/_2$ tsp. basil
$1/_8$ tsp. white pepper
Sliced almonds

Easy

Serves 4
May prepare ahead
Preparation time:
 20 minutes
Cook 20 minutes

Combine broccoli, onions and broth. Heat to boiling and simmer 5 minutes. Turn into blender jar and blend smooth. Melt butter and blend in flour. Stir in broccoli mixture, half and half, salt, basil, and pepper. Heat slowly, just to boiling. Simmer one minute, stirring. Top each serving with sliced almonds.

Chilled Tomato Soup

Easy

Serves 4
Prepare ahead
Preparation time:
 15 minutes
Chill 2–3 hours

3 medium ripe tomatoes
2 Tbsp. thinly sliced scallions
1 Tbsp. chopped fresh parsley
$\frac{1}{2}$ cup tomato juice
2 cups buttermilk
Salt and pepper to taste

Core tomatoes. Plunge into boiling water for one minute. Cool a little, then peel. Purée in food processor or blender with scallions, parsley, salt and pepper. Stir in juice and buttermilk. Chill 2–3 hours before serving.

Cold Squash Soup

Easy

Serves 6
Prepare ahead
Preparation time:
 40 minutes
Chill several hours

$1\frac{1}{2}$ lb. yellow squash, sliced
4 onions, chopped
$2\frac{1}{2}$ cups chicken stock, seasoned
1 cup sour cream
Salt, pepper and fresh dill to taste

In saucepan place squash, onions, and 2 cups of chicken stock. Bring to a boil; simmer until soft, about 30 minutes. Purée mixture in blender; transfer to a bowl. Stir in remaining stock, sour cream, salt and pepper. Chill, covered, for several hours. Garnish with fresh dill and serve.

Corn Chowder

3   cups water
3   cups diced potatoes
$^1/_2$ cup chopped onion
$^1/_2$ cup diced celery
$^1/_2$ tsp. dried basil
1   large bay leaf
1   16 oz. can cream-style corn
1   cup canned kernel corn
1   cup evaporated milk
1   cup 2% milk
1   cup canned tomatoes,
     drained and chopped
$^1/_2$ tsp. salt
$^1/_4$ tsp. pepper
Cornstarch (optional)

Easy

Serves 8
May prepare ahead
Preparation time:
* 30 minutes*
Cook 15–30 minutes

Combine first six ingredients in a large Dutch oven and bring to a boil. Reduce heat and simmer until potatoes are tender (about 10 minutes). Discard bay leaf. Stir in corn, milk, tomatoes, salt and pepper. Heat thoroughly, but do not boil. If you like chowder a little thicker, mix 1 Tbsp. cornstarch with 1 Tbsp. water and add to chowder.

Cream of Chicken Soup

Moderate

Serves 10–12
Preparation time:
2 hours
Cook 2 hours

Broth:
2½ lb. chicken parts
1   leek, sliced lengthwise
3   cups carrots, sliced
2   stalks celery with leaves
1   Tbsp. salt
1   Tbsp. parsley
¼   tsp. thyme
¼   tsp. marjoram
5   peppercorns
5   cups water

Soup:
5–6 cups broth
½   cup milk
1½ cups half-and-half
2   tsp. chives, snipped
½   tsp. dried tarragon, crumbled
½   cup butter, softened
½   cup flour
3   cups cubed chicken
1   cup halved snow pea pods
½   cup julienned carrots
Sharp cheddar cheese, grated

Place broth ingredients in a 5-quart kettle. Boil, reduce heat and cover. Simmer about 50 minutes, or until chicken is done. Remove chicken from bones, skin, and cube. Strain broth and discard cooked vegetables. Add milk, half-and-half, chives and tarragon to broth. Heat to boiling. Mix flour and softened butter to paste. Add 2 cups hot broth to flour and butter mixture. Stir flour, butter and broth mixture into remaining broth. Boil, reduce heat and simmer. Stir mixture until thickened. Blanch carrots and snow pea pods separately. Add chicken, carrots and pea pods just before serving. Sprinkle soup with grated cheese.

Fish Chowder

4 Tbsp. butter or margarine
1 cup celery, diced
$^1/_2$ cup onion, diced
$1^1/_2$ lb. frozen fish chunks or fillets
2 cans cream of potato soup
1 soup can water
$1^1/_2$ soup cans milk
1 Tbsp. chopped parsley
Salt and pepper to taste

Easy

Serves 6
May prepare ahead
Preparation time:
 10 minutes
Cook 30 minutes

Melt butter in large pot. Sauté celery and onion until tender. Add frozen fish; simmer 5 minutes. Break fish into bite-sized pieces. Add remaining ingredients; simmer 20–30 minutes.

Fabulous Lentil Soup

Easy

Serves 8
May prepare ahead
Preparation time:
15 minutes
Cook 1 hour

Freezes well

2	Tbsp. Crisco® oil
3	medium onions, chopped (about 2 cups)
3	carrots, coarsely grated
$^3/_4$	tsp. marjoram, crumbled
$^3/_4$	tsp. thyme leaves, crumbled
1	28 oz. can whole tomatoes, chopped coarsely, keep juice
7	cups beef broth ($3^1/_2$ cups canned, plus $3^1/_2$ cups water)
$1^1/_2$	cups dried lentils, rinsed
$^1/_2$	tsp. salt
$^1/_2$	tsp. black pepper
6	oz. dry white wine
2	Tbsp. dried parsley
4	oz. grated cheddar cheese (optional)

Heat oil in large saucepan and sauté onions, carrots, marjoram, and thyme for five minutes, stirring frequently. Add tomatoes with juice, broth, and lentils. Bring soup to a boil, reduce heat, cover, and simmer for one hour, until the lentils are tender. Add salt, pepper, wine, and parsley, and simmer for a few minutes. Top with cheese if desired.

Hot or Cold Tomato Soup

1½ sticks butter
2 Tbsp. olive oil
1 large onion, thinly sliced
½ tsp. thyme
½ tsp. basil
Salt and pepper
2½ lb. tomatoes, peeled, or a 2 lb. can
    Italian plum tomatoes
3 Tbsp. tomato paste
¼ cup flour
¾ cup chicken broth
1 tsp. sugar
1 cup heavy cream or half-and-half

Easy

Serves 8–12
May prepare ahead
Preparation time:
  15 minutes
Cook 30 minutes

Heat one stick of butter and oil together. Add onions, thyme, basil, salt and pepper. Cook until onion is wilted. Add tomatoes and tomato paste. Blend and cook 10 minutes. Put flour in bowl and blend with some of the broth until smooth. Stir into tomato mixture. Add rest of broth and simmer 30 minutes, stirring frequently. Put in blender and blend until smooth. Strain and return to heat. Add sugar and cream and simmer 5 minutes. Add remaining butter. Add cream just before serving.

Hearty Borscht

Easy

Serves 6
May prepare ahead
Preparation time:
 30 minutes
Cook 50 minutes

3   Tbsp. butter
1   onion, chopped
1   tsp. salt
1   tsp. caraway seeds
8   small beets, peeled and thinly sliced
1   carrot, thinly sliced
2   stalks celery, chopped
3   cups cabbage, chopped
$^1/_2$ lb. beef shin, diced
6   cups beef broth
$1^1/_2$ cups red potatoes, thinly sliced
1   Tbsp. cider vinegar
1   Tbsp. honey
$^1/_2$ cup tomato paste
Salt and pepper to taste
Sour cream
Fresh dill

Melt butter in large kettle and add onion, salt and caraway seeds; sauté until onion is translucent. Add beets, carrot, celery and cabbage; sauté 5 minutes more. Add beef broth and potatoes; bring to a boil and simmer until vegetables are tender, about 15 minutes. Add vinegar, honey and tomato paste. Season to taste with salt and pepper, cover and simmer 30 minutes more. Serve hot, topped with sour cream and garnished with fresh dill.

Light Hearted
Cincinnati Chili

½   large onion, chopped
1   Tbsp. Crisco® oil
1   lb. ground turkey
1   15 oz. can caliente style chili beans
1   8 oz. can tomato sauce
½   cup water
1   Tbsp. chili powder
½   tsp. ground cumin
½   tsp. sugar
½   tsp. ground cinnamon
¼   tsp. allspice
Fresh ground black pepper

Sauté onion in oil in a large skillet until tender. Add turkey, stirring to crumble meat. Cook until no redness remains in the meat. Drain fat. Add beans and liquid, tomato sauce, water, and spices. Simmer gently, covered, for 30 minutes. Stir occasionally.

Easy

Serves 4
May prepare ahead
Preparation time:
 15 minutes
Cook 30 minutes

Freezes well

A family favorite

Minestrone

Easy

Yield: 3 quarts
Prepare ahead
Preparation time:
 30 minutes
Cook 2 hours

Freezes well

$^1/_4$ lb. soup meat or stew meat, small chunks
2   quarts hot water
$1^1/_2$ cups tomato juice
1   can black bean soup
6   bouillon cubes
1   16 oz. can kidney beans with sauce
1   cup diced turnips
1   cup diced carrots
1   cup diced celery
1   cup shredded cabbage
1   cup chopped scallions or green onions
1   tsp. basil
1   tsp. MSG (optional)
$^1/_2$ tsp. salt
$^1/_4$ tsp. fresh ground pepper
$^3/_4$ cup uncooked spaghetti
Grated Parmesan cheese

Brown meat in oil. Add rest of ingredients and spices, except spaghetti and Parmesan, to pot. Bring to a boil, reduce heat and simmer 1 hour. Break spaghetti into small pieces and add to soup. Cook another hour. Sprinkle grated Parmesan cheese on top when serving. Best when served the next day.

Portuguese Red Bean Soup

2	15 oz. cans kidney beans
1	small onion, sliced
1	clove garlic, chopped fine
1	large potato, diced
1	Tbsp. Crisco®
Salt to taste	
$\frac{1}{8}$	tsp. paprika
$\frac{1}{8}$	tsp. pepper
2	15 oz. cans tomato sauce
1	ring Portuguese or Italian sausage, sliced
2	quarts water
$\frac{1}{2}$	Tbsp. lemon juice
$\frac{1}{4}$	small head cabbage, chopped
$\frac{1}{2}$	cup macaroni
$\frac{1}{2}$	cup celery, chopped

Easy

Serves 10
May prepare ahead
Preparation time:
 15 minutes
Cook 2 hours

Cook beans, onions, garlic, and potatoes in hot shortening for 15 minutes. Add salt, paprika, and pepper. Add tomato sauce, sausage, water and lemon juice. Cook 2 hours. Add cabbage and macaroni and cook 15 minutes more.

Reno Red Chili

Moderate

Serves 6 –8
May prepare ahead
Preparation time:
 30 minutes
Cook 2¹/₄ hours

Freezes well

Puts Skyline to
shame.

6   lb. lean beef, cubed (as in round)
6   dry chili peppers
Black pepper to taste
³/₄   cup water
3   Tbsp. cumin
6   minced cloves garlic
1   Tbsp. oregano
¹/₂   cup beer
8   Tbsp. chili powder
3   medium onions, chopped
2   Tbsp. paprika
3   Tbsp. cider vinegar
2   15 oz. cans beef broth
1   cup tomatoes, stewed and puréed
2   Tbsp. masa flour

Stem and seed peppers (wear gloves). Simmer them in water for 30 minutes. Brown meat, adding black pepper to taste. Drain off all fat. Add chili powder, cumin, and garlic. Cook 30 to 45 minutes using as little liquid as possible; add pepper water as necessary. Meanwhile, brew oregano in cool beer. Put to side. After cooked, mash chili peppers and add to meat. Then add onions, beer/oregano mixture, paprika, vinegar, 1 can broth, and tomatoes. Simmer 45 minutes, stirring occasionally. Dissolve flour in remaining can of broth; add to chili and simmer 30 minutes. Check seasonings, add salt to taste, simmer 15 minutes more. Serve with sour cream or cheese of choice.

Vichyssoise

4 Tbsp. butter
4 leeks, white part only, cut fine
1 medium onion, chopped
4 cups canned clear chicken broth
2 sprigs parsley
2 small stalks celery, chopped
1 large potato, sliced thin
Salt and pepper to taste
$\frac{1}{4}$ tsp. curry powder
5 drops Worcestershire
2 cups heavy cream
Chives, dill or parsley for garnish

Easy

Serves 8
Prepare ahead
Preparation time:
* 15 minutes*
Cook 30 minutes
Chill several hours

Melt butter in 5 quart pan. Add leeks and onion. Cook very slowly until vegetables are tender but not brown. Add broth, parsley, celery, potato, salt and pepper, curry and Worcestershire. Cook until potatoes and celery are tender. Let cool, put through food processor or blender. Refrigerate for several hours. Just before serving, stir in cream. Sprinkle with chives, dill, or parsley.

White Bean Chowder

Easy

Serves 6
May prepare ahead
Preparation time:
 5 minutes
Cook 1 hour

1½ cups white beans
1   tsp. garlic powder
1   medium onion, finely chopped
1   medium carrot, finely chopped
6   Tbsp. butter
1   bouquet garni
1   ham bone
¼   tsp. savory
¼   tsp. rosemary
1   tsp. parsley
1   bay leaf
5   cups chicken stock
¾   cup heavy cream

Soak beans overnight. Drain. Sauté garlic, onion, and carrot in butter. Add beans, bouquet garni, ham hock, and other spices, along with chicken stock. Simmer one hour or until beans are tender. Remove bouquet garni and bay leaf. Purée beans in food processor and return to soup. Stir cream into soup until well blended.

Asparagus Vinaigrette

2   lb. fresh asparagus, cooked
     (must be still green and firm)
$^1/_2$ cup Crisco® oil
4   Tbsp. wine vinegar
$^1/_2$ tsp. salt
$^1/_2$ tsp. dry mustard
$^1/_2$ tsp. chopped onion
1   Tbsp. pimiento
Leaf lettuce
4   slices bacon, fried and crumbled

Easy

Serves 6–8
May prepare ahead
Preparation time:
* 15 minutes*
Marinate 30 minutes

Arrange asparagus in flat, shallow dish. Combine oil, vinegar, salt, mustard, onion and pimiento. Pour half of dressing over asparagus and cover dish. Marinate in refrigerator 30 minutes. Arrange on lettuce and pour rest of dressing over top. Sprinkle bacon over all.

Bombay Salad

Easy

Serves 8
Prepare ahead
Preparation time:
 30 minutes
Chill 3 hours

An excellent summer
salad with cold beer
or iced Chinese tea.

$1^{1}/_{2}$ cups cold cooked rice
4   cups diced or shredded cooked chicken
1   cup diced celery
1   tsp. lemon juice
$^{3}/_{4}$ cup cottage cheese
$^{1}/_{2}$ cup sour cream
3   Tbsp. mayonnaise
$^{1}/_{2}$ tsp. salt
$^{1}/_{4}$ tsp. pepper
3   Tbsp. curry powder
$^{1}/_{2}$ cup raisins
1   8 oz. can mandarin oranges (drained)
$^{1}/_{2}$ cup peanuts

Combine rice, chicken and celery in a large bowl. Mix together the lemon juice, cottage cheese, sour cream, mayonnaise and spices. Add to chicken mixture. Add raisins, oranges, and peanuts. (Note: if preparing ahead, save peanuts until just before serving. Otherwise they will become soggy.) Chill at least 3 hours. Serve with traditional curry condiments: chutney, bananas, raita, toasted coconut.

California Salad
with Tarragon Dressing

¹/₂	cup mayonnaise
¹/₄	cup Crisco® oil
1	Tbsp. lemon juice
1	Tbsp. tarragon vinegar
1¹/₂	tsp. Worcestershire sauce
1¹/₂	tsp. soy sauce
2	tsp. crushed dried tarragon
¹/₄	tsp. pepper
1	large clove garlic, crushed
4	cups torn lettuce
2	cups sliced mushrooms
1	11 oz. can mandarin oranges, drained
1	avocado, cut in pieces
¹/₂	cup slivered almonds, toasted

Easy

Serves 4–6
*Partially prepare
 ahead*
*Preparation time:
 15 minutes*
Chill several hours

*Delicious and
attractive*

In a small bowl, use a wire whisk to combine mayonnaise, oil, lemon juice, tarragon vinegar, Worcestershire sauce, soy sauce, tarragon, pepper, and garlic. Cover and chill for several hours. At serving time, place lettuce on serving plates. Add the sliced mushrooms, avocado pieces, and orange sections. Spoon dressing over salad. Garnish with the slivered almonds.

Chicken and Tortellini Salad

Easy

Serves 8–10
Partially prepare
  ahead
Preparation time:
  2 hours

Excellent summer
main dish

4   whole chicken breasts,
      skinned, boned, cooked
14   oz. tortellini
2   cups broccoli
1   pint cherry tomatoes
4   oz. Italian salad dressing
6–8 oz. creamy Italian dressing
Salt and pepper to taste

Cook chicken breasts. Cut in chunks and re-frigerate to cool. Cook pasta, drain and cool. Cut up broccoli and put in boiling salted water for one minute. Drain and cool. Combine chicken, pasta, cherry tomatoes, and broccoli. Add Italian dressing. Just before serving add creamy Italian dressing. Salt and pepper to taste. Serve with fresh fruit and bread sticks.

Chicken and Wild Rice Salad

$^1/_2$ cup wild rice (uncooked)
$1^1/_2$ cups water
Salt
2   cups cooked chicken, diced
1   cup snow pea pods, 1" pieces
$^1/_2$ cup thinly sliced green onion
$^1/_2$ cup diced celery
$^1/_2$ toasted almonds, chopped

Tarragon Vinaigrette:
$^1/_2$ cup olive oil
$^1/_4$ cup white wine vinegar
1   tsp. dried tarragon
1   tsp. coarse salt
$^1/_2$ tsp. black pepper

Easy

Serves 4
Prepare ahead
Preparation time:
 50 minutes
Chill 2–3 hours

Rinse rice under running water. Bring $1^1/_2$ cups salted water to boil. Stir in rice and bring to boil again. Reduce heat and simmer 25–35 minutes until rice bursts open. Rinse rice under cold water and drain well. Put rice in bowl. Add chicken, snow peas, onion, celery, and almonds. Mix well.

Tarragon Vinaigrette:
Whisk oil and vinegar. Stir in tarragon, salt and pepper. Pour sparingly over chicken and rice. Toss gently; chill 2–3 hours.

Chicken Salad For One

Easy

Serves 1
May prepare ahead
Preparation time:
  10 minutes

1   cup cooked chicken
¹/₄   cup mayonnaise
¹/₄   cup cole slaw dressing
¹/₈   tsp. curry powder
6–8 seedless grapes
3   mandarin orange sections,
         pineapple chunks, or other fruit
3   tsp. sliced celery
Toasted, slivered almonds

Combine all ingredients except almonds. Refrigerate until ready to serve. Top with almonds before serving. If doubling this recipe, cut down slightly on the mayonnaise and cole slaw dressing.

Chunky Chicken Salad Casserole

1   small green pepper, sliced
$\frac{1}{4}$ cup skim milk
$\frac{1}{4}$ cup mayonnaise
1   2 oz. jar sliced pimientos
1   4 oz. can mushrooms, drained and sliced
$\frac{1}{2}$ cup slivered water chestnuts
2   cups cubed, cooked chicken
$\frac{1}{2}$ tsp. salt
1    $3\frac{1}{2}$ oz. can french fried onion rings

Easy

Serves 6
Partially prepare
 ahead
Preparation time:
 15 minutes
Bake 20 minutes

Preheat oven to 350°. Simmer green pepper slices in water until nearly tender;   drain. Combine milk with mayonnaise, add pimiento, green pepper, mushrooms, water chestnuts, chicken and salt. Place in a 1-quart casserole and top with onion rings (can be prepared ahead to this point). Cover and bake at 350° for 15 minutes. Remove cover and bake 5 minutes longer to crisp onion rings.

Cold Wild Rice Salad

Easy

Serves 6–8
Preparation time:
25 minutes

1	box long grain and wild rice
$\frac{1}{2}$	cup chopped celery
$\frac{1}{2}$	cup chopped green pepper
$\frac{1}{2}$	cup diced water chestnuts
$\frac{1}{2}$	cup sliced almonds, toasted
1	8 oz. can mandarin oranges
1	cup green grapes
$\frac{1}{3}$	cup olive oil

Salt and pepper

Cook rice according to directions. Cool completely. Add remaining ingredients, adjusting to taste. Toss gently. Serve at room temperature.

Copper Pennies

2   lb. carrots, sliced into $1/_4$ inch rounds
2   red onions, sliced and separated
1   green pepper, thinly sliced
1     $10\,^3/_4$ oz. can tomato soup
$^3/_4$ cup vinegar
$^2/_3$ cup sugar
$^1/_2$ cup Crisco® oil
1   tsp. Worcestershire sauce
1   tsp. prepared mustard
$^1/_2$ tsp. salt

Easy

Serves 10 –12
Prepare ahead
Preparation time:
* 20 minutes*
Marinate several
* hours*

Great for picnics.

Cook carrots until tender. Drain. Combine with onion and green pepper. Stir remaining ingredients; pour over vegetables. Cover and marinate in refrigerator for several hours or overnight.

A Different Caesar Salad

Easy

Serves 6
Preparation time:
 15 minutes

It's anchovy-less!

1   head romaine lettuce
1   clove garlic
3   Tbsp. olive oil
1   tsp. dried mustard
1   raw egg
1   lemon
Parmesan cheese
4   strips cooked bacon, crumbled
Croutons

Wash and dry lettuce. Rub salad bowl with clove of garlic that has been sliced in half. Leave some small pieces of garlic in bowl. Add olive oil and dried mustard. Mix with spoon. Tear lettuce and toss until coated. Break raw egg into salad. Toss well. Squeeze lemon and toss again. Sprinkle with Parmesan cheese. Toss well. Garnish with bacon and croutons.

Fresh Broccoli Salad

1 head raw broccoli,
  chopped in large bite-size pieces
½ cup mayonnaise
½ cup sugar
½ cup raisins
1 chopped onion (red or white)
8–10 slices cooked bacon, crumbled
1 Tbsp. vinegar
2 cups shredded cheddar cheese

Easy

Serves 6
May prepare ahead
Preparation time:
  1 hour
Chill 2–3 hours

Mix mayonnaise, sugar, raisins, onion, bacon, vinegar, and cheese. Pour over uncooked broccoli. Mix well and chill.

Frozen Fruit Salad

Easy

Yield: 15–16 individual molds
Prepare ahead
Preparation time: 20 minutes
Freeze several hours

Freezes well

A very versatile recipe

1   29 oz. can apricots with syrup
1   cup sugar
1   15 oz. can crushed pineapple with juice
3   bananas, diced
2   10 oz. pkg. frozen strawberries, thawed, with juice
1   Tbsp. lemon juice
Optional: fresh strawberries and whipped cream, or mayonnaise dollops for garnishing

Drain off syrup from apricots into sauce pan. Add sugar and simmer 5 minutes, then cool. Cut apricots into small pieces into large mixing bowl. Add other fruits with juices and lemon juice and cooled apricot syrup. Spoon into individual molds and freeze several hours. Remove from molds. Flash re-freeze. Remove to freezer bags. Let sit at room temperature 15 minutes before serving.

Grandma's Thanksgiving Cranberry Salad

Mold:
1   small can crushed pineapple, reserving liquid
Water
1   small box cherry gelatin
1   can whole berry cranberries
$\frac{1}{2}$ cup peeled and chopped apples
$\frac{1}{2}$ cup chopped nuts and/or celery
Lettuce leaves

Topping:
8   oz. cream cheese
$\frac{1}{2}$ tsp. vanilla
Milk (to desired consistency)
Confectioner's sugar (to taste)

Mold:
Drain pineapple juice from can and add enough water to equal 1 cup. Boil and dissolve gelatin, stirring until mixed. Add can of cranberries. Mix with mixer slightly until combined, but not crushed or chopped. Stir in by hand pineapple, chopped apples, and nuts and/ or celery. Pour in individual molds and chill several hours. When ready to serve, place molds on lettuce.

Topping:
Soften cream cheese. Add vanilla, then milk, and confectioner's sugar to taste and to the consistency you like.

Moderate

Serves 8
Prepare ahead
Preparation time:
 30 minutes
Chill several hours

Greek Salad

Easy

Serves 6
Partially prepare
 ahead
Preparation time:
 15 minutes

Healthy, elegant, and
delicious, too!

Dressing:
$^1/_4$ cup plus 1 Tbsp. olive oil
$^1/_4$ cup red wine vinegar
$^1/_2$ tsp. oregano
$^1/_2$ tsp. salt
$^1/_4$ tsp. pepper

Salad:
3 large tomatoes
1 cucumber, sliced
1 medium green pepper, diced
1 small onion, sliced
8 pitted ripe olives
2 heads Romaine lettuce
$^2/_3$ cup feta cheese, crumbled

Prepare dressing ahead: Combine olive oil and red wine vinegar; add oregano, salt and pepper. Prepare rest of salad ingredients, except cheese. Toss with dressing and feta cheese before serving.

Hawaiian Chicken Salad

3	cups chicken, cooked and cubed
$\frac{1}{4}$	cup chopped onion
1	cup chopped celery
1	cup mandarin oranges
4	tsp. chutney
$\frac{1}{4}$	cup sour cream
$\frac{1}{2}$	cup almonds
$\frac{1}{2}$	cup sliced water chestnuts
$\frac{1}{2}$	cup mayonnaise
1	cup pineapple chunks, drained

Mix all ingredients. Chill 30 minutes.

Easy

Serves 8
Prepare ahead
Preparation time:
 30 minutes
Chill 30 minutes

Served at 1988
JLC House Tour
Luncheon

Hot Chicken Salad for a Crowd

Easy

Serves 6–8
Partially prepare
  ahead
Preparation time:
  20 minutes
Bake 25 minutes

8   cups cooked chicken, cubed
6   cups diced celery
1   cup almonds
4   Tbsp. onion, grated
4   Tbsp. lemon juice
6   hard boiled eggs, chopped
2   tsp. salt
4   shakes Tabasco
2   cups mayonnaise
1   can cream of chicken soup
2   small cans water chestnuts, sliced
Pepper to taste
2   cups cheddar cheese, grated

Grease two 9x13 Pyrex dishes. Mix all ingredients together except cheese. Divide mixture between dishes. Top with grated cheese. Bake at 375° for 25 minutes.

Jeweled Chicken Salad

4	chicken breasts	*Easy*
1	cup sour cream	
4	Tbsp. mayonnaise	*Serves 4*
5	slices of bacon, cooked and crumbled	*Prepare ahead*
3	stalks of celery, chopped	*Preparation time:*
1	cup white, seedless grapes, halved	*45 minutes*
		Chill 1 hour

Cook chicken breast for ten minutes in boiling water, cool, debone and dice. Mix sour cream and mayonnaise. Add mayonnaise mixture to chicken, bacon, celery and mix well. Fold in grapes. Cool in refrigerator for at least one hour before serving.

Marinated Tuna and Vegetables

12½	oz. can water-packed tuna, drained	*Easy*
1	cup raw broccoli florets	
1	cup sliced carrots	*Serves 6*
1	cup raw cauliflower florets	*Prepare ahead*
1	cup celery, diagonally sliced	*Preparation time:*
1	cup fresh mushrooms, sliced	*10 minutes*
½	cup vinaigrette	*Marinate 8 hours or*
		overnight

Mix all ingredients together. Marinate in refrigerator 6–8 hours or overnight.

Oriental Tuna Salad

Easy

Serves 4–6
May prepare ahead
Preparation time:
   20 minutes

1   6 oz. pkg. frozen pea pods
1   12¹/₂ oz. can tuna, packed in water
1   cup celery, cut diagonally into small pieces
1   8 oz. can water chestnuts, drained and
    sliced
1   Tbsp. lemon juice
¹/₂ cup mayonnaise
1¹/₂ tsp. soy sauce
Garlic powder to taste
1   cup chow mein noodles

Thaw pea pods. Combine tuna, celery, water
chestnuts, and pea pods. Combine lemon
juice, mayonnaise, soy sauce, and garlic
powder. Pour over and mix into tuna mixture.
Cover and chill until serving. Mix in noodles
just before serving.

Pasta Salad

1   lb. colored rotini
1   small jar capers
1   bottle Marzetti® Caesar dressing (8 oz.)
2   16 oz. cans artichoke hearts
2   6 oz. cans ripe olives
1   medium red onion
1   large yellow pepper
1   large red pepper
1   large green pepper
1–1$\frac{1}{2}$ lb. Provolone or mozzarella cheese
Chopped parsley

Easy

Serves 10–12
Prepare ahead
Preparation time:
 30 minutes
Chill overnight

Served at the 1988
JLC House Tour
Luncheon

Night before:
Cook rotini. Add capers (drained). Add Marzetti® dressing. Let sit overnight in refrigerator.

Next day:
Add artichoke hearts, cut in large dice; ripe olives, sliced; red onion, cut in large dice; peppers, cut in large dice. Add cheese cut into squares. Mix all together. Add chopped parsley.

Pasta Salad Primavera

Easy

Serves 8
Prepare ahead
Preparation time:
 1 hour
Chill several hours

Dressing:
$1/2$ cup olive or Crisco® oil
$1/4$ cup fresh lemon juice
$1/2$ tsp. salt
Fresh ground pepper
2 Tbsp. fresh chives, cut
1 tsp. dried basil
$1/2$ tsp. dried dill weed

Pasta:
8 oz. rotelle or other pasta

Vegetables:
$1/2$ lb. broccoli, cut into flowerets
$1/2$ red pepper, cut into $1/4$ inch strips
$1/2$ green pepper, cut into $1/4$ inch strips
$1/4$ lb. fresh snow pea pods, ends trimmed
$1/2$ pint cherry tomatoes
6 large pitted black olives, sliced
$1/4$ cup chopped parsley

Garnish:
$1/2$ lb. large shrimp in the shell, cooked,
 shelled, cleaned and chilled.
 Chicken may be substituted.

In a jar with a tight lid, combine dressing ingredients. Shake well. Cook pasta as directed on the label until it is just done. Drain and rinse with cold water. Drain well. Pour into salad bowl and toss with dressing. Steam broccoli, peppers and pea pods in a small amount of water for 3 to 4 minutes, just until heated through and color is set. Drain and rinse with cold water. Drain well. Add to pasta along with tomatoes, olives and parsley and toss until well coated with dressing. Chill several hours before serving. At serving time toss again and garnish with shrimp or chicken.

Salad Soufflé

1	8 oz. can crushed pineapple
1	3 oz. pkg. orange Jello®
$^3/_4$	cup boiling water
$^3/_4$	cup mayonnaise
1	cup finely shredded cabbage
1	cup finely shredded carrots
$^1/_2$	cup raisins
$^1/_2$	cup chopped walnuts
3	egg whites, beaten stiffly

Bibb lettuce leaves

Moderate

Serves 6–8
May prepare ahead
Preparation time:
  1 hour
Chill 1 hour

Fold 22 inch piece of foil in half lengthwise. Tape around 1 quart soufflé dish. Drain pineapple, reserving liquid. Dissolve Jello® in boiling water. Add reserved pineapple liquid. Beat in mayonnaise. Pour into loaf pan and freeze until soft in center and firm around edges; about 20 minutes. In a large bowl, beat Jello® mixture until fluffy. Fold in pineapple and next 4 ingredients, then egg whites. Pour into prepared soufflé dish. Chill until set. Serve on lettuce leaves.

Salade Niçoise

Easy

Serves 10–12
Partially prepare
 ahead
Preparation time:
 1 hour

Salad:
1   head Bibb lettuce, torn (2 cups)
3   cups torn Romaine lettuce
1   7 oz. can tuna, drained and
    broken into chunks
1   10 oz. pkg. French string beans, cooked,
    drained and chilled
1   cup cherry tomatoes, halved
1   small green pepper, cut in rings
1   small red onion,
    sliced and separated into rings
3   hard boiled eggs, chilled and
    cut into wedges
1   medium potato, cooked, chilled and diced
$1/_2$ cup olives

Dressing:
1   cup Crisco® oil
$1/_3$ cup vinegar
$1/_3$ cup lemon juice
2   tsp. sugar
$1^1/_2$ tsp. salt
$1^1/_2$ tsp. paprika
$1^1/_2$ tsp. mustard
$1/_2$ tsp. oregano, crushed
Dash cayenne pepper

Salad:
Spin salad greens and combine them in a large salad bowl. Add tuna, beans, tomatoes, pepper, onion, eggs, potato and olives. Be sure to drain and spin all liquids from lettuce, tuna, beans and olives. Add desired amount of dressing, toss to coat well.

Dressing:
Combine all ingredients. Cover and shake.
Chill. Shake again just before serving.

Seafood Pasta Salad

1	lb. vermicelli
1/2	cup green pepper, chopped
2	cups celery, chopped
3	eggs, hard boiled and chopped
2	oz. pimiento
10	green onions
3/4	cup almonds, slivered
1 1/2	lb. shrimp (frozen salad shrimp)
1 1/2	lb. crabmeat or imitation crab
2	pkg. ranch dressing

Easy

Serves 8
Prepare ahead
Preparation time:
 20 minutes
Chill overnight

Break pasta into small pieces and cook until just tender. Drain. Combine pasta, green pepper, celery, eggs, pimiento, onions, and almonds. Refrigerate 24 hours. Before serving prepare ranch dressing. Mix pasta mixture, dressing, and add seafood; let stand 1 hour before serving.

Sour Cream Potato Salad

Easy

Serves 8
Prepare ahead
Preparation time:
 40 minutes
Chill overnight

3 lb. new potatoes
1 cup mayonnaise
1 cup sour cream
$^1/_2$ minced onion
1 cup chopped celery
2 Tbsp. white vinegar
3 chopped hard boiled eggs
Salt and pepper to taste
Dash paprika

Boil potatoes until tender. Mix together mayonnaise, sour cream, onion, celery, vinegar, and chopped eggs; add to potatoes. Season with salt and pepper. Refrigerate overnight. Sprinkle with paprika.

Spinach Salad

Salad:

1   lb. fresh spinach, torn
1   can bean sprouts, drained
1   can water chestnuts, thinly sliced
8   slices cooked bacon, crumbled
4   hard cooked eggs, diced

Dressing:

1   cup Crisco® oil
³/₄ cup sugar
¹/₃ cup catsup
¹/₂ tsp. salt
1   medium onion, quartered
1   Tbsp. Worcestershire sauce
¹/₄ cup vinegar

Layer salad in large bowl. In blender, blend ingredients for dressing. Add to spinach just before serving and toss gently.

Easy

Serves 8
Partially prepare
 ahead
Preparation time:
 30 minutes

Spinach Salad with Poppyseed Dressing

Easy

Serves 10
Partially prepare
 ahead
Preparation time:
 30 minutes

Dressing can be
stored in refrig-
erator 2 weeks.

1 lb. fresh spinach, torn
1 large can Mandarin oranges, drained
1 lb. cooked bacon, torn into pieces
4–6 hard boiled eggs, sliced

Dressing:
1 scant cup Crisco® oil
³/₄ cup sugar
¹/₂ cup vinegar
1 medium onion, chopped
1 tsp. dry mustard
2 tsp. poppy seeds

Combine salad ingredients and set aside or refrigerate. Combine dressing ingredients in a jar. Shake well. Add to salad just before serving.

82

Strawberry Spinach Salad

1   lb. spinach, washed and torn
1   quart strawberries
1   Tbsp. poppy seeds
2   Tbsp. sesame seeds

Dressing:
$^1/_2$ cup sugar
$^1/_4$ cup tarragon vinegar
$^1/_2$ cup olive oil
$1^1/_2$ Tbsp. minced onion
$^1/_4$ tsp. paprika

Mix salad ingredients in bowl. Mix dressing in blender. Pour over salad. Toss before serving.

Easy

Serves 6–8
Partially prepare ahead
Preparation time: 30 minutes

Sumi Salad

Easy

Serves 4–6
Prepare ahead
Preparation time:
  30–45 minutes
Chill several hours
  or overnight

2   Tbsp. Crisco® oil
¹/₂   cup sliced almonds
¹/₄   cup sesame seeds
1   head cabbage, finely chopped,
     or 1¹/₂ pkg. chopped cabbage
8   green onions, sliced
2   3 oz. pkg. Ramen® noodles,
     uncooked and broken into pieces

Dressing:
³/₄   cup Crisco® oil
6   Tbsp. rice vinegar
1   tsp. dry mustard
2   Tbsp. soy sauce

Heat oil in skillet, sauté almonds and sesame seeds until lightly browned. Combine with cabbage, onions, noodles and dressing. Cover and chill several hours or overnight.

Summery Salad

1	head Boston lettuce
1	cucumber
2	tomatoes
1	green pepper
$\frac{1}{2}$	avocado
5	radishes
1	peach
2	slices pineapple
1	4 oz. can Mandarin oranges
$\frac{1}{4}$	lb. fresh strawberries

Dressing:

1	small onion, minced
2	tsp. prepared mustard
6	Tbsp. lemon juice
$\frac{1}{4}$	tsp. salt
$\frac{1}{8}$	tsp. white pepper
3	Tbsp. Crisco® oil
1	sprig parsley, chopped
$\frac{1}{2}$	tsp. dried dill weed
$\frac{1}{4}$	tsp. dried tarragon
$\frac{1}{4}$	tsp. dried basil

Wash, peel, dice (or slice) all fruits and vegetables. Arrange in a large bowl. To make dressing, blend all ingredients in blender. Correct seasonings if needed. Pour over salad, mix gently but thoroughly. Cover and let salad marinate 10 minutes.

Easy

Serves 6–8
Partially prepare
* ahead*
Preparation time:
* 20–30 minutes*
Marinate 10 minutes

Tomato Aspic

Easy

Serves 8
Prepare ahead
Preparation time:
  10–15 minutes
Chill 2–3 hours

Garnish with sliced hard boiled eggs, and serve with mayonnaise.

2   cups V-8® juice
1   small pkg. lemon gelatin
Lettuce

Boil one cup V-8® juice. Add to gelatin, stir until dissolved. Add one cup cold V-8® juice. Chill until set. Serve on bed of lettuce.

Waldorf Chicken Salad

Easy

Serves 12
May prepare ahead
Preparation time:
  10 minutes

Serve in pita sandwiches or on a bed of lettuce.

$^2/_3$ cup mayonnaise
$^2/_3$ cup unflavored yogurt
6   cups cooked chicken
2   cups diced red apple
1$^1/_2$ cups sliced celery
$^3/_4$ cup raisins
6   Tbsp. chopped walnuts
6   Tbsp. sliced green onions
Salt to taste

Mix mayonnaise and yogurt. Add remaining ingredients; toss to blend thoroughly.

Creamy Raspberry Dressing

²/₃ cup mayonnaise
2   Tbsp. raspberry vinegar
4   tsp. sugar
1   tsp. salt

Mix all ingredients in bowl until sugar dissolves.

Easy

Yield: ²/₃ cup
May prepare ahead
Preparation time:
* 5 minutes*

Parmesan Cheese Dressing

2–4 cloves fresh garlic, minced
¹/₂   tsp. pepper
¹/₄   tsp. dry mustard
1   Tbsp. lemon juice
¹/₄   cup Crisco® oil
3   Tbsp. grated Parmesan cheese
Salad greens for 4

Put garlic, pepper and mustard in salad bowl. Mix with a fork and add lemon juice, oil, and cheese. Heap greens enough for 4 on top of dressing, but do not toss yet. Chill until meal time. Before serving, toss greens in dressing until coated.

Easy

Serves 4
Prepare ahead
Preparation time:
* 10 minutes*
Chill at least
* 30 minutes*

This dressing is great with mixed greens, especially romaine

Vinaigrette Dressing

Easy

Yield: 1¹/₂ cups
May prepare ahead
Preparation time:
 5 minutes

³/₄ cup Crisco ® oil
¹/₄ cup olive oil
³/₄ cup red wine vinegar
1 Tbsp. sugar
1 tsp. salt
1 tsp. garlic powder
2 cloves garlic
1 tsp. Dijon mustard
¹/₂ tsp. ground pepper
¹/₂ tsp. chopped parsley
¹/₂ tsp. oregano
¹/₂ tsp. basil
1 tsp. lemon juice

Combine all ingredients in food processor or blender. Refrigerate.

Meats

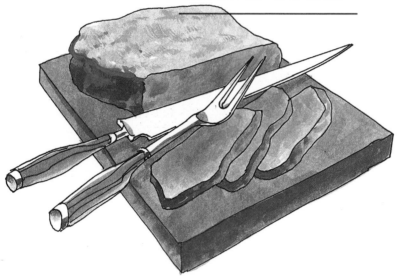

Beef Brisket in Beer

3–4 lb. beef brisket
Salt and pepper to taste
1   onion, sliced
$^1/_4$ cup chili sauce
2   Tbsp. brown sugar
1   clove garlic, minced
1   12 oz. can (1$^1/_2$ cups) beer
2   Tbsp. all-purpose flour

Easy

Serves 8–10
May prepare ahead
Preparation time:
 10 minutes
Bake 4 hours

Freezes well

*Delicious with but-
tered noodles or a
noodle Kugle*

Trim excess fat from brisket. Season with salt and pepper. Place meat in a 13x9x2 baking dish; cover with onion slices. In bowl, combine chili sauce, brown sugar, garlic and beer. Pour over meat. Cover with foil. Bake in 350° oven for 3$^1/_2$ hours. Uncover and bake 30 minutes more, basting with juices. Remove meat to platter. Skim excess fat from drippings. Measure liquid and add water to make one cup. Blend flour and $^1/_2$ cup water; combine with drippings in saucepan. Cook, stirring constantly over medium heat until thickened and bubbly. To serve cut meat across grain; pass gravy.

Beef in Herb Wine Sauce

Moderate

Serves 8
Preparation time:
 15 minutes
Cook 2¹/₂ hours

3-4 medium onions, sliced
2 Tbsp. bacon drippings
2 lb. lean beef (sirloin tip)
1 cup beef bouillon
1¹/₂ cups dry red wine
¹/₂ lb. fresh mushrooms
¹/₄ cup butter
1¹/₂ Tbsp. flour
¹/₄ tsp. thyme
¹/₄ tsp. oregano
¹/₄ tsp. marjoram
1 tsp. salt
¹/₂ tsp. pepper

Cut beef into 1¹/₂" cubes. Sauté onions in bacon drippings until yellow. Remove from pan and set aside. Add meat cubes, sprinkle lightly with flour and brown meat thoroughly. When meat is browned add ³/₄ cup beef bouillon, 1 cup red wine and the herbs and seasonings. Cover pan tightly and simmer over low heat (or in 300° oven) about 2 hours; gradually add remaining bouillon and wine. Sauté mushrooms in ¹/₄ cup butter. Add onions and mushrooms and cook 20-30 minutes longer until meat is tender.

Beef Marinade

1	cup olive oil
$\frac{1}{2}$	cup red wine
2	garlic cloves, finely chopped
4	green onions with tops , finely chopped
12	peppercorns, crushed
1	bay leaf
$\frac{1}{2}$	tsp. oregano
$\frac{1}{2}$	tsp. basil
$\frac{1}{4}$	tsp. salt

Blend all ingredients and use to marinate 4 hours or more.

Easy

Yield: $1\frac{1}{2}$ cups
Prepare ahead
Preparation time:
*   15 minutes*

Beef Stew

2	lb. stew beef
3	russet potatoes, peeled
6	onions, peeled and halved
4	carrots, peeled and cut into chunks
3	Tbsp. minute tapioca
1	15 oz. can tomato sauce
1	15 oz. can burgundy wine

Mix all ingredients well. Bake covered at 250° for 5 hours.

Easy

Serves 6
May prepare ahead
Preparation time:
*   15 minutes*
Bake 5 hours

This melts in your mouth. Great served with buttered noodles, salad and bread.

Brisket

Easy

Serves 6
Prepare ahead
Preparation time:
 5 minutes
Bake 4-6 hours

Freezes well

This recipe may be cooking while you are sleeping, chill during the day. Slice and reheat for dinner.

1   15 oz. can jellied cranberry sauce
1   envelope onion soup mix
$^{1}/_{4}$ cup catsup
4   oz. cola
4   lb. brisket of beef

Mix first four ingredients, set aside. Bake brisket uncovered at 475° without the sauce for $^{1}/_{2}$ hour. Remove from oven, pour sauce over meat, reduce heat to 275°. Cover tightly with 2 layers of aluminum foil and cook 4-6 hours. Chill in juices. Slice when cold. Put into serving dish with juices to reheat. Cover with foil and heat for 45 minutes at 350°. If you choose to cook this while sleeping, cook brisket at 225° for 8 hours.

Chateaubriand

Easy

Serves 8
Prepare ahead
Preparation time:
 15 minutes
Chill 10–12 hours,
 marinate 2 hours
Roast 25 minutes.

Good for elegant dinner or cocktail buffet. Serve with stuffed mushrooms and a salad.

3–4 lb. beef tenderloin
1   Tbsp. thyme
1   tsp. white pepper
1   Tbsp. seasoned salt
1   tsp. garlic salt
$^{1}/_{4}$ tsp. oregano
$^{1}/_{4}$ cup Worcestershire sauce

Place beef on large sheet of aluminum foil and rub thyme into beef. Sprinkle with mixture of white pepper, seasoned salt, garlic salt and oregano. Wrap and refrigerate 10–12 hours. Place in cooking pan and sprinkle with $^1/_4$ cup Worcestershire sauce. After 2 hours add 1 cup water. Cook at 400° for 20–25 minutes for very rare.

Easy Marinade

$^3/_4$ cup French dressing
$^3/_4$ cup soy sauce
2   Tbsp. sesame seeds (optional)
Flank steak or pork tenderloin

Mix French dressing and soy sauce. Pour over meat. Sprinkle with sesame seeds. Marinate overnight or at least several hours. Grill to taste.

Easy

Yield: 1$^1/_2$ cups
May prepare ahead
Preparation time:
  10 minutes
Marinate at least
  3 hours

Serve hot in winter or cold in summer. Can be grilled a day or two ahead, sliced and served cold with salad and cold pasta.

Fillets of Beef Chasseur

Difficult

Serves 8
May prepare ahead
Preparation time:
 45 minutes
Bake 15-20 minutes

Great for a crowd.
This dish benefits
from being prepared
a day ahead.

8	filet mignon steaks (6–8 oz. each)
1	large clove garlic, crushed
1½	tsp. seasoned salt
¼	tsp. pepper
6	Tbsp. butter
2	Tbsp. brandy
3	Tbsp. flour
2	tsp. tomato paste
½	tsp. crushed garlic
¾	cup dry red wine
1	cup chicken broth
½	cup beef broth
¼	tsp. Worcestershire sauce
2	Tbsp. currant jelly
½	lb. mushrooms, sliced

Place steaks on a work surface. In a small bowl, make a paste of the garlic, seasoned salt and pepper. With hands, rub seasonings on both sides of steaks. Heat 2 Tbsp. butter in a large heavy skillet (not non-stick) until very hot. Sauté 4 steaks at a time over moderately high heat until brown on each side but still raw in the middle (add more butter as needed). Put steaks in a 9x13 casserole, leaving 1 inch between steaks. Add brandy to skillet. Cook over moderate heat, stirring constantly, scraping up all brown bits. Add ½ stick butter. When melted and foamy, stir in flour. Reduce heat to low and cook, stirring constantly until mixture is golden. Stir in tomato paste and garlic. The mixture will be thick and grainy. Remove pan from heat and whisk in wine, chicken and beef broths. Return to moderate heat and bring to a boil, stirring constantly. Reduce heat and simmer for 10 minutes, stirring occasionally or until reduced by a third. Stir in Worcestershire and currant jelly. When jelly melts, stir in mushrooms and adjust seasonings. If sauce is too thick, thin down with water, broth or wine. Cool completely. Pour over steaks in casserole. Sauce should come only half way up steaks. At this point steaks may be covered with foil and refrigerated overnight. Before serving, bring to room temperature about 2 hours. Preheat oven to 400°. Bake uncovered 15–20 minutes for medium-rare, 20–25 minutes for medium-well.

Flank Steak Marinade

¹/₄ cup soy sauce
¹/₄ cup Crisco® oil
1 tsp. celery salt
2 tsp. chopped green onion
1 clove garlic, minced
1 tsp. lemon pepper
1 Tbsp. lemon juice

Easy

Yield: ¹/₂ cup
May prepare ahead
Preparation time:
 10 minutes
Marinate at least
 4 hours

Mix all ingredients. Marinate flank steak at least 4 hours or overnight. Grill or broil as desired.

Glazed Corned Beef

Moderate

Serves 8 –10
Partially prepare
  ahead
Preparation time:
  10 –15 minutes
Cook 2 hours

Sauce can be cooked
and beef can be
boiled a day ahead

2	cups red currant jelly
$\frac{1}{2}$	cup ruby port
$\frac{1}{2}$	cup chopped shallots
$\frac{1}{4}$	cup fresh lemon juice
$4\frac{1}{2}$	tsp. grated lemon peel
1	Tbsp. orange peel
1	Tbsp. dry mustard
$1\frac{1}{2}$	tsp. ground ginger
$1\frac{1}{2}$	tsp. ground pepper
$\frac{1}{2}$	tsp. salt
3	lb. corned beef
$\frac{1}{2}$	cup coarse grain mustard
$\frac{1}{2}$	cup brown sugar, packed

Combine first 10 ingredients and heat in sauce pan over medium-low heat until jelly melts. Boil corned beef according to package directions, less 15–20 minutes. Drain and spread with mustard. Pour $2\frac{1}{2}$ cups sauce over beef. Sprinkle with brown sugar. Bake at 350° for 45 minutes, basting occasionally. Pass remaining sauce.

Greek Stew

3½ lb. cubed beef (1½" cubes)
Salt and fresh ground pepper
¼ cup butter
2½ lb. small, peeled onions
1 6 oz. can tomato paste
¾ cup dry red wine
2 Tbsp. red wine vinegar
1 Tbsp. brown sugar
1 clove garlic, minced
1 bay leaf
1 small cinnamon stick
½ tsp. whole cloves
¼ tsp. ground cumin
2 Tbsp. currants or raisins

Season meat with salt and pepper. Melt butter in a large dutch oven. Add meat and coat with butter, but do not brown. Arrange onions over meat. Mix together all other ingredients and pour over meat and onions. Cover and simmer gently, or bake covered in a 300° oven, until meat is very tender, about 3 hours. If baking, more wine may be added if necessary.

Easy

Serves 6
May prepare ahead
Preparation time:
 15 minutes
Cook 3 hours

A favorite for cold and snowy nights. Serve with rice.

London Broil Teriyaki

Easy

Serves 4-6
Partially prepare
ahead
Preparation time:
10 minutes
Marinate 4 hours
to 2 days
Grill 8-10 minutes

Delicious every time

³/₄	cup Crisco® oil
¹/₄	cup soy sauce
2	Tbsp. red wine vinegar
¹/₄	cup honey
2	Tbsp. finely chopped green onions
1	clove garlic, minced
1¹/₂	tsp. ground ginger
1¹/₂	lb. flank steak

Combine all ingredients, except steak, in a large bowl. Mix well. Score the flank steak on both sides. Put steak in baking pan and pour marinade over. Marinate at least 4 hours in refrigerator. (Can be done up to 2 days in advance.) Grill over medium coals 4-5 minutes each side for medium rare. Slice on the diagonal and serve.

Meatballs

1	lb. ground beef
2	eggs, beaten
2	Tbsp. chopped parsley
2	Tbsp. Parmesan cheese
$^1/_2$	cup seasoned bread crumbs
1	garlic clove, minced
$1^1/_2$	tsp. salt
$^1/_8$	tsp. pepper
2	Tbsp. Crisco® oil

Mix all ingredients and form into balls. Fry in oil and drain on paper. Add to your favorite sauce.

Easy

Serves 8
May prepare ahead
Preparation time:
 10 minutes
Cook 10 minutes

Freezes well

Saucy Oven Barbecued Steak

Easy

Serves 4
Partially prepare
  ahead
Preparation time:
  20 minutes
Bake 1 hour

2   lb. boneless round steak
1   Tbsp. Crisco® oil
³/₄ cup ketchup
¹/₂ cup water
¹/₂ cup cider vinegar
1   Tbsp. brown sugar
1   Tbsp. prepared mustard
1   Tbsp. Worcestershire sauce
¹/₂ tsp. salt
¹/₈ tsp. pepper

Trim excess fat from steak. Cut into serving size pieces. Heat oil in a large skillet; add steak and brown on both sides. Transfer steak to a 2 quart shallow baking dish. Combine remaining ingredients, stirring well; pour over steak. Cover and bake at 350° for 1 hour or until tender.

Sauerbraten

Marinade:
Equal amounts cider vinegar and water
    (about 2 cups each)
$\frac{1}{2}$ lemon, sliced
2   Tbsp. sugar
1   Tbsp. salt
2   medium onions, sliced
6   bay leaves
12 whole cloves
16 whole black peppercorns

$3\frac{1}{2}$ lb. cross rib roast, rump or pot roast
20 gingersnaps, crushed

Mix marinade; add meat. Marinate at least 2–3 days, turning meat every 12–24 hours. Take meat out of marinade; strain liquid and reserve. Brown meat, then add liquid and crushed gingersnaps. Simmer for 2 hours. Thicken gravy with flour if needed.

Easy

Serves 8
Partially prepare
* ahead*
Preparation time:
* 10 minutes*
Marinate 2–3 days
Cook 2 hours

Texas Fajitas

Easy

Serves 4-6
Partially prepare
ahead
Preparation time:
 10 minutes
Marinate 8 hours
Grill 8–10 min-
utes

Strips of chicken
breast make a fine
variation

$^1/_2$ cup lime juice
$^1/_4$ cup tequila
3-4 cloves garlic, minced
1 large onion, sliced
1 4 oz. can whole green chilies,
 sliced lengthwise
$^1/_4$ cup Crisco® oil
$^1/_2$ tsp. bottled hot pepper sauce
$^1/_4$ tsp. salt

$1^1/_2$ lb. skirt or flank steak
Flour or corn tortillas
Sliced avocado
Sour cream
Grated cheese
Salsa Picante (next recipe)
Chopped onions
Chopped tomatoes

Mix first 8 ingredients well. Place steak in zip-lock bag or large glass baking dish; pour marinade over. Marinate in refrigerator 8 hours (may be marinated up to 48 hours ahead). Cook on mesquite grill until medium rare (about 8–10 minutes). Slice thinly; serve with tortillas and side items for make-your-own fajitas.

Texas Fajitas
Salsa Picante

1   16 oz. can stewed tomatoes or 3 large ripe tomatoes, peeled and cut into quarters
1   clove garlic
1   onion, quartered
2   Tbsp. vinegar or lemon juice
1   tsp. salt
¼   cup fresh cilantro (optional)
2   pickled or fresh jalapeno peppers, or to taste

Combine all ingredients except jalapenos in food processor; process until coarsely chopped. Add jalapenos one at a time; taste after each addition to suit individual taste. Serve with fajitas or any Mexican dish.

Easy

Yield: 2 cups
May prepare ahead
Preparation time:
  20 minutes

Freezes well

Spicy Flank Steak

Easy

Serves 4
Partially prepare
  ahead
Preparation time:
  10 minutes
Marinate 8-24 hours
Grill 10 minutes

$\frac{1}{2}$ cup catsup
$\frac{1}{2}$ cup water
$\frac{1}{4}$ cup lemon juice
2   tsp. Worcestershire sauce
1   bay leaf
1   tsp. pepper
$\frac{1}{4}$ tsp. crushed basil
1   tsp. celery seeds
Dash of Tabasco
2–3 lb. flank steak

Combine all ingredients except steak. Simmer over low heat for 10 minutes. Cool. Marinate flank steak 8-24 hours. Grill over medium heat for 8-10 minutes.

Barbecued Butterflied Leg of Lamb

1   6 lb. leg of lamb, butterflied by
     your butcher
½   cup Dijon mustard
2   Tbsp. soy sauce
1   clove garlic, mashed
1   tsp. dried rosemary
¼   tsp. ground ginger

Combine all ingredients except leg of lamb. Paint lamb with mixture. Let sit for several hours in the refrigerator. Cook over medium high coals, one half hour on each side for medium rare. Slice thinly and serve. For oven cooking instead, bake 350° for 1-1¼ hours in a roasting pan.

Easy

Serves 8
*Partially prepare
  ahead*
*Preparation time:
  15 minutes*
*Refrigerate several
  hours*
Grill 1 hour

*Unusual and easy
way to prepare
lamb*

Fål Kål

Easy

Serves 6–8
May prepare ahead
Preparation time:
 30 minutes
Cook 2–3 hours

A Norwegian recipe
for the lamb and
cabbage lover

2–4 lb. lamb (breast or shoulder)
4–8 lb. cabbage
1–2 Tbsp. butter
Salt
Flour
1   tsp. peppercorns

Cut lamb breast or shoulder into suitable serving pieces. Cut cabbage into rectangular pieces about 1 inch thick. Melt some butter (1–2 Tbsp.) in heavy skillet or Dutch oven. Remove from heat; sprinkle flour over butter. Place alternate layers of cabbage and lamb, sprinkling each layer with salt, a little flour and a few peppercorns. Pour boiling water over lamb and cabbage until it covers one third of contents. Simmer slowly 2–3 hours, stirring occasionally so that it won't burn.

Lamb Chops Deluxe

$^1/_4$ lb. blue cheese
1   tsp. salt
Dash of pepper
1   tsp. Worcestershire sauce
8   lamb chops, 2" thick
1   10 $^3/_4$ oz. can consommé
Watercress for garnish (optional)

In small bowl with fork, mix cheese, salt, pepper, and Worcestershire until blended and creamy. Spread mixture evenly over fatty sides of chops. In 13x9 baking dish arrange chops, standing on bones, apart from each other. Add undiluted consommé. (To bake at a later time, refrigerate at this time.) Bake uncovered at 325° for 40 minutes for medium rare, basting occasionally. To serve, arrange chops on large platter, garnish with watercress. Strain consommé through fine strainer. Serve with chops.

Easy

Serves 8
Partially prepare
 ahead
Preparation time:
 5 minutes
Cook 40 minutes

Extremely elegant and super simple! The sauce can be made 1 hour before serving or early in the day.

Lamb Curry

Easy
Serves 4–6
May prepare ahead
Preparation time:
  15 minutes
Cook 45 minutes

Freezes well

This mild curry dish is a hit with young and old. It keeps beautifully–if you have any left over.

1	onion, chopped
1	clove garlic, crushed
4	Tbsp. butter
2	stalks celery, chopped
1	small green apple, chopped
3	Tbsp. minced candied ginger
$\frac{1}{2}$	tsp. chili powder
2	tsp. tomato paste
1	Tbsp. flour
$1\frac{1}{2}$	Tbsp. curry powder
3	cups chicken stock
3	cups seedless raisins
3	cups diced cooked lamb

Salt and pepper to taste

Rice for 6 servings

Condiments:
Chutney
Hard boiled eggs, chopped
Crumbled bacon
Chopped peanuts
Grated coconut

Sauté onion and garlic in butter until golden. Add celery, green apple, ginger and chili powder. Cook until all vegetables are soft. Make a roux of tomato paste, flour and curry powder and add to above mixture. Stir in slowly 3 cups chicken stock. Add raisins and lamb. Simmer covered over low heat for 45 minutes or until sauce is reduced. Serve with rice and condiments

Sour Cream & Herb Lamb

6   lb. leg of lamb, boned, defatted,
     and butterflied
$^1/_2$ tsp. pepper
1   cup sour cream
3   cloves garlic, minced
2   Tbsp. chopped fresh parsley
1   tsp. dried rosemary
1   tsp. dried oregano
1   tsp. salt

Place lamb on baking sheet. Combine all remaining ingredients. Spread over all surfaces of the lamb. Cover loosely with waxed paper. Refrigerate at least 4 hours or up to two days. Bring to room temperature before cooking (1 hour). Prepare grill or preheat broiler. Barbecue or broil lamb until instant reading thermometer inserted in thickest part of the meat registers 130° to 140° for rare or 160° for medium. (This will take 45 minutes to 1 hour.) Let rest at room temperature for 10 minutes. Cut thin slices across grain of meat.

Easy

Serves 6
Partially prepare
*   ahead*
Preparation time:
*   15 minutes*
Marinate 4 hours to
*   2 days*
Grill 45 minutes to
*   1 hour*

This tastes best if grilled rather than broiled

Lamb Marinade

Easy

Yield: 1 cup
Prepare ahead
Preparation time:
15 minutes

$^2/_3$ cup olive oil
$^1/_3$ cup lemon juice
2   garlic cloves, finely chopped
$^1/_4$ cup parsley, minced
Salt and pepper

Blend all ingredients together. Marinate lamb 3 hours or more.

Apple Raisin Sauce

Easy

Yield: 2 cups
May prepare ahead
Preparation time:
10 minutes
Cook 15–20 minutes

Serve with baked ham, pork chops or roast pork

2   Tbsp. light brown sugar
2   Tbsp. cornstarch
$^1/_2$ tsp. dry mustard
2   Tbsp. melted butter
2   cups apple cider
1   cup raisins

Blend sugar, cornstarch and mustard with melted butter. Gradually add cider; heat, stirring constantly, until thickened and smooth. Add raisins and cook over medium heat stirring occasionally for 15–20 minutes.

Cherry Sauced Pork Loin

1 4 –5 pound pork loin roast, boned, rolled and tied
1/2 tsp. salt
1/2 tsp. pepper
Dash dried thyme, crushed

Sauce:
1 cup cherry preserves
1/4 cup red wine vinegar
2 Tbsp. light corn syrup
1/4 tsp. ground cinnamon
1/4 tsp. ground nutmeg
1/4 tsp. ground cloves
1/4 tsp. salt
1/4 cup toasted slivered almonds

Easy

Serves 10–12
Preparation time:
* 15 minutes*
Roast 3 hours

Rub roast with mixture of salt, pepper and thyme. Place on rack in 13x9x2 baking pan. Roast uncovered in slow oven, 325°, for about 2¹/₂ hours. Meanwhile combine cherry preserves, vinegar, corn syrup, cinnamon, nutmeg, cloves and salt. Heat to boiling, stirring occasionally; reduce heat, simmer 2 minutes and add toasted almonds. Spoon sauce over roast and continue roasting 30 minutes longer or until thermometer registers 170°. Pass sauce with meat.

Chinese Spare Ribs

Easy

Serves 4
Partially prepare
  ahead
Preparation time:
  5 minutes
Bake 1 hour and
  45 minutes

Freezes well

6   Tbsp. soy sauce
6   Tbsp. granulated sugar
6   cloves crushed garlic
3   lb. spare ribs

Mix soy sauce, sugar and garlic. Set aside. Bake ribs 45 minutes at 375° with no sauce on them. Drain off fat. Reduce heat to 350°. Pour sauce over ribs. Baste every 15 minutes for 1 hour.

Curry-Spiced Pork Kebobs

2 lb. pork tenderloin
1 medium onion, quartered
3 medium red peppers, cut into large pieces
$\frac{1}{2}$ cup bottled steak sauce
$\frac{1}{4}$ cup Crisco® oil
2 Tbsp. curry powder
3 Tbsp. ketchup
1 tsp. lemon peel
$\frac{1}{2}$ tsp. salt
$\frac{1}{2}$ cup melted apple jelly ($\frac{1}{2}$ of 10 oz. jar)

Easy

Serves 4–6
*Partially prepare
  ahead*
*Preparation time:
  15 minutes*
*Marinate at least
  1 hour*
Grill 35–40 minutes

Cut meat into 2" cubes. Combine meat, onions and peppers with remaining ingredients except apple jelly. Cover and refrigerate at least one hour, stirring occasionally. Thread meat, onion and peppers alternately on 6 skewers, reserving marinade. Cook over medium heat on grill for 35–40 minutes or until pork is tender. Brush often with marinade and turn occasionally. Brush kebobs with melted jelly; cook one minute longer.

Holiday Ham

Moderate

Serves 6
Prepare ahead
Preparation time:
 20 minutes
Chill sauce overnight
Bake 1¹/₂ hours

Holiday Ham:
10–12 lb. boneless smoked ham
Whole cloves
4   Tbsp. Dijon mustard
1   garlic clove, mashed
¹/₄ cup Chinese duck sauce (plum sauce)
Dash orange juice
¹/₂ cup brown sugar

Mustard Sauce:
¹/₄ cup dry English mustard
¹/₂ cup tarragon vinegar
1¹/₂ Tbsp. dark rum
3   eggs
6   Tbsp. sugar
4   Tbsp. unsalted butter
¹/₂ tsp. salt
Pinch freshly ground pepper

Heat oven to 400°. With a sharp knife, score top of entire ham. Stud with cloves at every intersection. Combine the mustard, garlic, and duck sauce with enough orange juice to make a syrupy mixture. Spread evenly over top and sides of ham. Sprinkle surface of ham with brown sugar and bake 1¹/₂ hours. Serve warm or at room temperature.

Mustard Sauce:

Place dry mustard in a bowl; add vinegar and rum. Do not stir. Cover and let stand in refrigerator overnight. Place mustard mixture in double boiler over hot water and whisk until well blended. Add eggs, one at a time, whisking vigorously after each addition. Gradually whisk in sugar until smooth. Beat in butter, salt, and pepper. Cook until thick, about 5 minutes. Do not overcook or eggs will curdle.

Ham and Asparagus Casserole

Moderate

Serves 12
May prepare ahead
Preparation time:
* 1 hour*
Bake 30 minutes

Good for a winter
luncheon or
weekend supper.

2¼ lb. cooked ham
1½ lb. fresh asparagus
¾   lb. pasta
½   cup butter
½   cup flour
3   cups light cream
1½ cups milk
½   cup chicken broth
½   cup sharp cheddar cheese, grated
½   cup Parmesan cheese, grated
½   cup grated onions
2   tsp. prepared mustard
2   Tbsp. minced fresh parsley
1½ tsp. salt
⅛   tsp. pepper
1   cup mayonnaise

Cut ham into ½ inch cubes. Steam asparagus in salted water until barely tender. Drain and cool. Cut into 1½ inch pieces. Cook pasta according to package directions. Rinse and drain. Melt butter in saucepan. Blend in flour. Blend in cream, milk and broth. Cook sauce until thickened, stirring constantly. Stir in cheeses. Season sauce with onions, mustard, parsley, salt, rosemary and pepper. Stir in mayonnaise. Preheat oven to 350°. Layer half each of the ham, asparagus, pasta and sauce in a buttered 4 quart casserole. Repeat layers. Bake uncovered for 30 minutes or until bubbly.

Orange-Soy Marinade For Pork Loin

3/4 cup orange juice
2 Tbsp. soy sauce
1 tsp. sugar
1 clove garlic, minced
1 tsp. pepper
1/2 tsp. thyme

Mix all ingredients. Pour over pork loin. Marinate at least two hours. Grill over medium coals 20 minutes per pound.

Easy

Yield: 3/4 cup
Partially prepare
ahead
Preparation time:
10 minutes
Marinate at least
2 hours

Oriental Tenderloin

Easy

Serves 4–6
Partially prepare
  ahead
Marinate several
  hours or overnight
Preparation time:
  10–15 minutes
Bake 45 minutes to
  1 hour

$^1/_2$ cup soy sauce
1   Tbsp. grated onion
1   large clove garlic
1   Tbsp. vinegar
$^1/_2$ tsp. vinegar
$^1/_4$ tsp. pepper
$^1/_2$ tsp. sugar
2   1$^1/_4$ lb. pork tenderloins
4   bacon strips

Combine soy sauce, onion, garlic, vinegar, pepper and sugar. Marinate tenderloins several hours or overnight, turning several times. Remove from marinade, place in roasting pan and cover each tenderloin with two bacon strips. Bake at 325° for 45 minutes to one hour, basting several times with the reserved marinade.

Pork Roast
with Apple Topping

4–5 lb. pork loin roast
2   Tbsp. flour
1   tsp. dry mustard
1¹/₂ tsp. salt
¹/₂ tsp. sugar
¹/₄ tsp. black pepper
¹/₄ tsp. ground sage

Topping:
1¹/₂ cups sliced apples (Granny Smith are best)
¹/₂ cup brown sugar
¹/₄ cup apple juice
¹/₄ tsp. cinnamon
¹/₄ tsp. mace
¹/₄ tsp. salt

Mix flour, salt, mustard, sugar, pepper, and sage together. Rub mixture over surface of pork. Place fat side up in the roasting pan. Bake for 1¹/₂ hours at 325°. Mix all of the topping ingredients together. Pour over roast. Bake 1 hour longer. Let stand for 10 minutes and serve.

Easy

Serves 6
Partially prepare
  ahead
Preparation time:
  20 minutes
Roast 2 ¹/₂ hours

Sausage and Lima Beans Provençale

Moderate

Serves 6
May prepare ahead
Preparation time:
 30 minutes
Cook 1 hour

Freezes well

6	large sweet Italian sausages
2	cups dry white wine
1	large onion, chopped
4	cloves garlic, pressed
1	16 oz. can plum tomatoes, drained and chopped
1	bay leaf
$\frac{1}{2}$	tsp. basil
2	tsp. sugar
$\frac{1}{2}$	cup chicken broth
2	pkg. frozen lima beans
5	Tbsp. chopped fresh parsley

Place sausages in large heavy skillet. Add enough white wine to come halfway up the sides of the sausages. Bring to a boil, turn sausages and partially cover. Cook over medium heat until wine disappears and sausages begin to brown. When browned on all sides, remove to a plate and keep warm. Add onion and garlic and sauté until golden (add olive oil if necessary). Add tomatoes, bay leaf, sugar and basil and cook 5 minutes. Return sausages to pan and add $\frac{1}{2}$ cup more white wine and chicken broth. Cook 5 more minutes. Add lima beans and parsley and simmer for 30-45 minutes.

1¹/₄ lb. pork fillets
1 oz. clarified butter
  or 2 Tbsp. Crisco® oil and
  ¹/₂ oz. butter
2 shallots, chopped
1 Tbsp. paprika
1 Tbsp. flour
2¹/₂ oz. sherry
¹/₂ cup beef consommé
2 oz. mushrooms
4 Tbsp. cream

Easy

Serves 2
May prepare ahead
Preparation time:
  10–15 minutes
Cook 50 minutes

Cut the fillets in diagonal slices about ¹/₂ inch thick; sauté meat in small batches quickly in butter until colored. Remove and set aside. Add shallots and paprika to pan and cook 2–5 minutes. Stir in flour and add sherry and stock. Replace meat. Bring to a boil and simmer gently 30–40 minutes. Wipe and trim mushrooms; add to pan and continue cooking 10–15 minutes. Add the cream and adjust the seasoning and reheat.

Spicy Pork Loin

Easy

Serves 6
Partially prepare
  ahead
Preparation time:
  10 minutes
Marinate overnight
Grill 2 hours

5   large cloves fresh garlic, minced
2   tsp. paprika
$^1/_4$ cup crushed peppercorns
1   tsp. oregano
1   tsp. ground red pepper
$^1/_2$ cup Crisco® oil
4   lb. boneless center cut pork loin roast

In small bowl, combine seasonings. Add oil and rub mixture over pork. Cover with plastic wrap and refrigerate overnight. Use covered kettle grill. Arrange coals in a circle; put a drip pan beneath roast. Grill, turning roast occasionally until temperature of meat reaches 170°, approximately 2 hours. Let stand 10 minutes.

The Best Spare Ribs

2   cups sugar
$^1/_4$ cup paprika
1   Tbsp. garlic powder or to taste
2–3 racks of baby back ribs
1   cup apple cider vinegar
1   cup barbecue sauce mixed with 1 tsp. thyme, 1 Tbsp. liquid smoke and more garlic powder to taste

Line pan with aluminum foil. Mix sugar, paprika, and garlic in bowl. Cut spare ribs into individual ribs and rub in sugar mixture. Put on rack in pan, cover with aluminum foil and bake for 1 hour and 15 minutes at 375°. Drizzle cider vinegar over ribs, cover again and bake 15 minutes more. Remove cover, slather on barbecue sauce mixture and bake for another 20–30 minutes.

Easy

Serves 4
Partially prepare ahead
Preparation time: 10 minutes
Bake 2 hours

Serve with sauerkraut

Cold Veal Stuffed with Ham, Liver, and Pistachios

Difficult

Serves 10–12
Prepare ahead
Preparation time:
  1 hour
Roast 2 hours
Chill 2 hours

Perfect for a
summer buffet
supper

3   lb. top cut leg of veal, in one piece
¹/₂   lb. calves' liver
³/₄   lb. cooked ham
¹/₂   cup finely chopped pistachio nuts
1   tsp. salt
¹/₂   tsp. allspice
¹/₄   tsp. thyme
3   Tbsp. minced onion
Dash fresh ground pepper
¹/₂   cup melted butter
Flour, salt, pepper
5   strips salt pork

Pound veal as thin as scaloppine. Drop calves' liver in boiling water for 10 minutes, then grind, being careful to remove all gristle and membrane. Grind cooked ham. Mix ham and liver together with pistachio nuts. Season with salt, allspice, thyme, minced onion and ground pepper. Add melted butter and mix well. Spread mixture over the surface of the veal and roll tightly as you would a jelly roll. Secure with string about every 3 inches. Dust the veal with flour, salt and pepper. Lay strips of salt pork over veal and roast in an uncovered baking pan in a 325° oven for 2 hours or until 180° on meat thermometer. Chill well and remove string before slicing.

Geschnetzeltes
(Swiss Julienne of Veal)

2 lb. boneless veal cutlets, $^1/_3$ inch thick
Salt, pepper and paprika to taste
3 Tbsp. butter or margarine
2 Tbsp. chopped shallots or green onions
3 Tbsp. flour
1 cup whipping cream
$^1/_2$ cup dry white wine
1 cup sliced mushrooms (optional)
$^1/_4$ cup brandy

Put 1 piece of meat at a time between two sheets waxed paper and pound with mallet to flatten evenly to $^1/_4$ inch thick. Sprinkle meat lightly on each side with salt, pepper and paprika to taste. Cut into $^1/_4$ inch x 1$^1/_2$ inch wide strips. Heat large frying pan and melt the butter until bubbly. Add shallots or green onions and sauté until just softened. Add veal strips and cook over medium-high heat until no longer pink (about 4 minutes). Remove meat to a bowl. Stir flour into pan drippings. Cook, stirring, until bubbly. Gradually blend in whipping cream and wine; cook stirring until thickened and smooth (add mushrooms if desired). If preparing ahead, cover, refrigerate the meat and sauce separately. Shortly before serving, add cooked meat to hot (or reheated) sauce in a chafing dish or other pan. Cook, stirring frequently (about 5 minutes). Heat $^1/_4$ cup brandy until warm to touch, ignite and pour over veal in sauce. Stir until flame dies down, then serve.

Moderate

Serves 6
May prepare ahead
Preparation time:
 10 minutes
Cook 20 minutes

Pronounced
Guh-shnet-sel-tis.

Accompany with rice or butter roasted potatoes.

Veal Scaloppine

Moderate

Serves 6
Partially prepare
* ahead*
Preparation time:
* 10 minutes*
Cook 20 minutes

24   2 oz. slices lean milk white veal
1   cup flour
4   Tbsp. butter
Salt and pepper to taste
4   oz. dry sherry
2   cups veal base or consommé
     or chicken broth
1   cup sliced cooked fresh mushrooms

Ask butcher to pound thin each slice of veal or do it yourself with a mallet between 2 sheets of waxed paper. Using two large skillets, melt 2 Tbsp. butter in each over a low fire. Dip the veal slices in flour and then brown in the pans, raising the fire. Brown lightly on one side, season with salt and pepper. Turn and do the same. Add 2 oz. sherry to each pan; let sherry reduce (boil down), then add ½ cup mushrooms to each pan. Add 1 cup veal base, consommé or chicken broth. Let simmer for 2 minutes. Serve 4 pieces per person, each with mushroom sauce.

Veal Scaloppine Marsala

¹/₃ stick butter
¹/₄ cup olive oil
Flour for dredging
2¹/₂ lb. veal scaloppine (¹/₄ inch thick,
     cut in 2 inch pieces)
1   cup sliced fresh mushrooms
1   cup stuffed green olives
¹/₄ cup Marsala wine

Melt butter and olive oil in frying pan. Flour meat lightly, saute 3–4 minutes (meat should be a light golden brown). Lower heat and add mushrooms, olives and wine. Simmer 7–10 minutes.

Easy

Serves 6
*Partially prepare
  ahead*
*Preparation time:
  10 minutes*
Cook 15 minutes

Poultry

Apricot Chicken and Stuffing

1 cup apricot preserves
$^1/_3$ cup dry white wine
$^1/_4$ cup butter or margarine, melted
2 8 oz. pkg. stuffing mix, prepared
$^3/_4$ cup pecans
6 chicken breast halves
Salt and pepper
Parsley

Easy

Serves 6
*Partially prepare
 ahead*
*Preparation time:
 20 minutes*
Bake 1 hour

Combine first three ingredients in small bowl. Set aside. Prepare stuffing mix according to package directions and stir in pecans. Spread in greased 9x13 baking dish. Wash chicken; pat dry. Season with salt and pepper. Brush chicken with apricot sauce and place on bed of stuffing. (Can be prepared ahead to this point.) Cover and bake at 350° for 30 minutes. Remove cover and bake additional 30 minutes. To serve, spoon remaining sauce over chicken and stuffing and garnish with sprig of parsley.

Brunswick Stew

1   4$\frac{1}{2}$–5 lb. hen, or 4 whole chicken breasts
      and 4 thighs
4   cups fresh corn, cut from the cob
4   cups fresh tomatoes (may use canned)
2   cups fresh or frozen lima beans
3   large onions, chopped
2   large potatoes, diced
$\frac{1}{4}$ cup lemon juice
$\frac{1}{4}$ cup cider vinegar
2   Tbsp. brown sugar
$\frac{1}{2}$ cup Worcestershire sauce
4   Tbsp. butter or margarine
1   tsp. Tabasco sauce, or more to taste
1   cup catsup
Pinch of cloves
2   cups okra, sliced

Cover chicken with water in large soup pot; add salt to season. Cook until tender. Remove chicken, reserving broth. Pull meat off bone and cut into small pieces. Return to pot and add all other ingredients, except okra, in order given. Cook slowly until thick, stirring often to prevent sticking. Taste to correct seasoning. Add okra; cook until okra is done.

Catalina® Chicken

6　whole, boneless, skinned chicken breasts (legs or wings can be used to make hors d'oeuvres)

1　8 oz. bottle of Catalina® salad dressing (low-cal if desired)

1　envelope onion soup mix

1　can cranberry sauce with whole cranberries

Split chicken breasts and arrange in a 9x13 glass casserole. Mix Catalina® dressing, onion soup and cranberry sauce. Pour over chicken. Bake at 325° for 1 hour 15 minutes.

Easy

Serves 6–8
May prepare ahead
Preparation time:
　15 minutes
Bake 1 hour and
　15 minutes

Chicken Artichoke Casserole

Moderate

Serves 2–4
Partially prepare
ahead
Preparation time:
20 minutes
Bake 30 minutes

Serve with wild rice
and spinach salad

1   2 lb. can artichoke hearts, drained and
    halved
4   cooked, cubed chicken breast halves
$\frac{1}{2}$ lb. fresh mushrooms
4   Tbsp. butter or margarine, divided
$2\frac{1}{2}$ Tbsp. flour
$\frac{1}{2}$ tsp. salt
$\frac{1}{4}$ tsp. pepper
Dash cayenne pepper
1   cup light cream
1   Tbsp. Worcestershire sauce
$\frac{1}{4}$ cup sherry
$\frac{1}{4}$ cup Parmesan cheese

Place drained and halved artichoke hearts in
buttered shallow baking dish (quiche pan is
perfect). Top with cooked chicken. Sauté
mushrooms in 2 Tbsp. of the butter. Add to
baking dish. Make cream sauce by melting
remaining butter in saucepan and stirring in
flour, salt, pepper, cayenne and cream. Stir
over low heat until smooth and thickened. Add
Worcestershire sauce and sherry. Stir until
mixed. Pour over casserole and sprinkle with
Parmesan cheese. (Can be prepared ahead to
this point.) Bake at 350° for 30 minutes (40
minutes if taken from the refrigerator.)

Chicken Italian

6	boned, skinned chicken breast halves
1/4	cup Italian salad dressing
1/4	tsp. thyme
1/4	tsp. oregano
1/2	tsp. basil
3	medium zucchini, quartered and sliced
1	large onion, chopped
1	small green pepper, chopped
1	16 oz. can tomatoes, chopped
1	8 oz. can tomato sauce
1/4	cup grated Parmesan cheese

Easy

Serves 8
May prepare ahead
Preparation time:
20 minutes
Bake 1 hour

Cube uncooked chicken breasts (about 5 cubes per half breast). Place chicken and remaining ingredients, except for cheese, in 13x9x2 casserole in the above order. Bake, covered, at 350° for 50 minutes to 1 hour, until chicken is cooked and zucchini is almost tender. Sprinkle with Parmesan cheese and continue baking, uncovered, about 10 minutes.

Chicken in Phyllo with Bechamel Sauce

1 lb. pkg. frozen phyllo dough
1 stick butter, melted

Filling:
1 stick butter
1 celery heart, finely chopped
3 medium onions, finely chopped
3–4 whole chicken breasts, cooked and finely
      cubed
1 cup chicken broth
2 Tbsp. chopped fresh parsley
Salt and pepper to taste
3 eggs, beaten until frothy

Bechamel Sauce:
$\frac{1}{4}$ cup butter
5 Tbsp. flour
$2\frac{1}{2}$ cups hot chicken broth
$1\frac{1}{4}$ tsp. salt
$\frac{1}{4}$ cup fresh lemon juice
3 beaten egg yolks

Thaw frozen phyllo dough, in package, in refrigerator overnight. Unroll carefully and cover with slightly damp linen towel or plastic wrap until ready to use. Set melted butter aside.

138

Filling:

Melt butter in skillet and sauté celery for five minutes. Add onion and continue cooking until onion is transparent. Add chopped chicken and broth, cook until liquid is absorbed. Remove from heat and cool. Add parsley, salt and pepper. Fold in beaten egg. Set aside.

Place phyllo dough on baking sheet. Brush each sheet with reserved melted butter until you have six sheets. Spread enough chicken mixture on dough to just cover entire surface, leaving two inches at edges. Roll up like a jelly roll. With seam side down, seal edges securely. Brush with butter. Slice $3/_4$ of the way through into eight equal portions. Prepare a second roll in the same way. Bake at 350° for 40 minutes or until golden. Prepare bechamel sauce during last five minutes of baking.

Bechamel Sauce:

Melt butter and add flour. Stir well over low heat for three minutes and add hot chicken broth all at once. Stir briskly. Add salt. Combine lemon juice and eggs in a separate bowl. Add a little sauce to the eggs, stir. Turn eggs into the sauce and stir thoroughly.

Place two portions of chicken/phyllo roll onto each plate and top with bechamel sauce.

Chicken Jubilee

1   16½ oz. can dark sweet cherries
¾   cup sherry
1   12 oz. bottle chili sauce
½   cup brown sugar
1   Tbsp. Worcestershire sauce
4   whole chicken breasts, halved
½   stick butter, melted
Salt and pepper

Drain cherries, reserving liquid. If thicker sauce is desired, thicken reserved cherry juice with 1 tsp. of cornstarch and add at end. Make mixture of chili sauce, brown sugar, Worcestershire sauce, sherry and cherries and set aside. Place chicken breast halves in 9x13 baking dish. Brush with melted butter. Season with salt and pepper. (Can be prepared ahead to this point.) Bake 45 minutes, uncovered, in 350° oven. Add sherry mixture. Bake, covered, 15–20 minutes longer.

Chicken Kiev Country Style

6	skinned, boned chicken breast halves
$\frac{1}{2}$	cup butter
$\frac{1}{2}$	cup fine dry bread crumbs
2	Tbsp. grated Parmesan cheese
1	tsp. oregano
1	tsp. basil
$\frac{1}{2}$	tsp. garlic salt
$\frac{1}{4}$	cup white wine
$\frac{1}{4}$	cup chopped green onion
$\frac{1}{4}$	cup chopped fresh parsley

Preheat oven to 375°. Melt butter. Combine bread crumbs, cheese, oregano, basil, and garlic salt. Dip chicken breasts in melted butter, then coat with crumb mixture and lay in 8x11 baking dish. (Can be prepared ahead to this point and refrigerated). Bake 40 minutes or until fork tender. Meanwhile, add wine, onion, and parsley to reserved melted butter. When chicken is golden brown, pour butter-wine sauce over chicken. Continue baking 3–5 minutes, to warm sauce.

Easy

Serves 4
Partially prepare
ahead
Preparation time:
20 minutes
Bake 40 minutes

Serve with wild rice and a pretty green salad

Chicken Pibil

Easy

Serves 4
May prepare ahead
Preparation time:
  15 minutes
Bake 1 hour

Freezes well

A great Mexican dish

4	skinned, boned chicken breast halves
4	large banana leaves or aluminum foil cut in four 12x18 pieces
1	Tbsp. chili powder
2	Tbsp. lemon or lime juice
1	medium onion, sliced
1	Tbsp. Crisco® oil

Place chicken on banana leaves or pieces of aluminum foil. Make paste of chili powder and lemon or lime juice and spread on chicken. Sauté sliced onion in oil until transparent. Lay several slices on each piece of chicken. Wrap chicken in leaves or aluminum foil, sealing edges. (Can be prepared ahead to this point.) Place in 9x13 baking dish and bake at 350° for 1 hour. Open foil or leaves carefully, allowing steam to escape, and serve.

Chicken, Artichokes and Mushrooms

Easy

Serves 4
Partially prepare
  ahead
Preparation time:
  25 minutes
Cook 25 minutes

4	boned, skinned chicken breast halves
	Flour, salt and pepper
$^1/_4$	cup butter
$^1/_2$	lb. whole, fresh mushrooms
$^1/_2$	cup dry white wine
1	14 oz. can artichokes, halved
$^2/_3$	cup chicken broth (optional)

Cut chicken into bite sized pieces. Dredge in flour. In large skillet, quickly brown chicken in $\frac{1}{4}$ cup butter. Add mushrooms and sauté. Add wine and simmer for one minute. Add artichoke hearts (and broth, if thinner sauce is desired). Cover and simmer 20 minutes.

To prepare ahead, transfer to 8x11 baking dish after addition of artichoke hearts and broth. Cool and refrigerate. Bake at 350°, covered, for 30 minutes.

Curry Chicken Delight

8   skinned, boned chicken breast halves
$\frac{1}{2}$ cup flour
4   slices bacon
$\frac{1}{4}$ cup honey
2   Tbsp. prepared mustard
$\frac{1}{2}$ tsp. salt
$\frac{1}{2}$ tsp. curry powder
Hot, cooked long grain rice

Easy

Serves 4
Preparation time:
 10 minutes
Bake 55 minutes

Great for a cool rainy evening. Cozy food!

Rinse chicken, pat dry. Coat chicken with flour; set aside. In skillet, cook bacon till crisp. Remove bacon, crumble, set aside. Reserve drippings. Add chicken to skillet and brown slowly in hot bacon drippings, about 10 minutes. Transfer chicken to 8x11 baking dish. Bake uncovered at 350° for 30 minutes. Combine honey, mustard, salt and curry powder. Drizzle over chicken, bake 15 minutes more. Top with bacon. Serve with rice.

Easy Cheesy Chicken

Easy

Serves 6–8
May prepare ahead
Preparation time:
15 minutes
Bake 1 hour

2   cups Parmesan cheese
Salt and pepper to taste
$^1/_2$ tsp. dried parsley
1   cup Ritz® cracker crumbs
4   whole chicken breasts, halved
1   stick melted butter
$^1/_2$ stick butter or margarine
$^1/_4$ cup lemon juice

Mix the Parmesan cheese, salt and pepper, parsley and cracker crumbs. Dip chicken in melted butter, then coat with above mixture. Place chicken in baking dish and dot with $^1/_2$ stick butter or margarine. Dribble lemon juice over all. Bake, uncovered, at 350° for 1 hour.

Herbed Chicken

Easy

Serves 6
May prepare ahead
Preparation time:
30 minutes

Bake 45 minutes

1   6 oz. pkg. long grain and wild rice
3   chicken breasts, halved and boned
Salt and pepper to taste
$^1/_4$ cup butter
1   10 oz. can condensed
       cream of chicken soup
$^3/_4$ cup sauterne
$^1/_2$ cup sliced celery
1   3 oz. can sliced mushrooms
1   Tbsp. diced pimiento

Prepare rice. Salt and pepper chicken and brown in butter. Spoon rice into 1½ quart casserole; top with chicken. Add soup to skillet; add sauterne, stirring until smooth. Add remaining ingredients; bring to a boil; pour over chicken. Cover. Bake at 350° for 25 minutes. Uncover; bake 15-20 minutes longer, until tender.

Honey Barbecued Broilers

2   broilers (2–2½ lb. each)
     or 3–4 lb. fryer chicken, cut up
¼   lb. butter
1   large shallot, peeled and sliced
¼   cup honey
¼   cup vinegar
2   tsp. salt
½   tsp. dry mustard
¼   tsp. dried marjoram

Easy

Serves 6
Preparation time:
 10 minutes
Bake 50 minutes

Place broilers skin side down in a 9x13 dish. Dot with ¼ lb. butter. Top chicken with shallot. Bake in 350° oven 30 minutes, until chicken starts to brown. Mix honey, vinegar, salt, mustard and marjoram, brush on chicken. After 10 minutes, pour remainder of sauce on chicken and bake 10 more minutes or until well browned.

Janie's Ohio Baked Chicken

Easy

Serves 4–6
*Partially prepare
  ahead*
*Preparation time:
  10 minutes*
Bake 1 hour

4–6 skinned and boned chicken breast halves
1   tsp. paprika
1   tsp. celery salt
1   tsp. curry powder
1   tsp. oregano
1¹/₂ tsp. salt
1¹/₂ tsp. freshly ground pepper
¹/₄ cup melted butter
1¹/₂ cups light cream
1   cup sliced almonds
¹/₂ cup sour cream

Put chicken breasts in one layer in 9x13 pan. Combine seasonings and mix well with melted butter. Pour over chicken. Top with light cream and almonds. Cover with aluminum foil. (Can be prepared ahead to this point.) Bake at 350° for 45 minutes. Uncover and stir sour cream into sauce. Bake uncovered 15 minutes more and serve.

Oriental Chicken Casserole

4	skinless, boneless chicken breast halves
$\frac{1}{2}$	cup butter
4	large carrots, julienned
1	can water chestnuts, sliced and drained
$\frac{1}{2}$	lb. fresh mushrooms, sliced
1	medium onion, chopped
1	cup dry white wine
$\frac{1}{4}$	cup cold water
2	Tbsp. cornstarch
2	cups chicken stock
$\frac{1}{2}$	tsp. thyme

Salt and pepper to taste

Easy

Serves 4
*Partially prepare
 ahead*
*Preparation time:
 30 minutes*
Bake 1 hour

*Serve over hot but-
tered noodles or
rice*

Cut chicken in bite sized pieces. In large skillet, brown chicken in 4 Tbsp. butter. Cover and simmer 10 minutes. Remove to large baking dish. Add remaining butter to skillet and sauté carrots, onion, water chestnuts and mushrooms for 5 minutes. Place in baking dish with chicken. Mix cornstarch with wine and water and pour into skillet. Add chicken broth and seasonings and cook until thickened. Pour sauce over chicken and vegetables and bake, covered, 45 minutes at 350°. Remove cover and bake additional 15 minutes.

To prepare ahead, follow all steps except baking. Refrigerate; add 15 minutes to baking time.

Oven Barbecued Chicken

Easy

Serves 4
May prepare ahead
Preparation time:
 5 minutes
Bake 1¹/₂ hours

Freezes well

1	chicken, cut up (or 4 breasts)
1	Tbsp. red wine vinegar
1	Tbsp. dark brown sugar
¹/₂	cup catsup
2	Tbsp. Worcestershire sauce
¹/₂	tsp. dry mustard
1	cup water
¹/₈	tsp. salt
¹/₂	onion, sliced
¹/₂	lemon, sliced

Place chicken in baking dish. Mix next seven ingredients and pour over chicken. Top with slices of onions and lemon. Bake at 350°, uncovered, for 1¹/₂ hours, basting often.

Parisian Chicken

Easy

Serves 10–12
May prepare ahead
Preparation time:
 30 minutes
Bake 30 minutes

1	quart sour cream
2	envelopes dry onion soup mix
4	pkg. frozen broccoli, cooked
4	cups cooked chicken
2	cups heavy cream, whipped
¹/₄	cup Parmesan cheese, grated

Mix sour cream and dry onion soup mix. Arrange cooked broccoli in a very large buttered casserole dish. Spoon half of the sauce over broccoli. Arrange chicken pieces over sour cream sauce. Add whipped cream to remaining sour cream mixture and spoon over all. Top with Parmesan cheese. Bake in 350° oven 30 minutes or until hot and bubbly.

Pecan Chicken

4   large skinless, boneless, chicken breast halves
1/2   cup buttermilk
1/4   cup Dijon mustard
Salt and pepper to taste
1   cup finely ground pecans

Easy

Serves 4
May prepare ahead
Preparation time:
  15 minutes
Refrigerate several
  hours
Bake 15 minutes

Serve with steamed vegetables

Pound the chicken between waxed paper sheets until one half inch thick. Combine buttermilk and mustard and season with salt and pepper. Coat chicken with mixture and refrigerate several hours or overnight. When ready to cook, preheat oven to 375°. Shake off excess buttermilk mixture and thoroughly coat each piece of chicken with ground pecans. Place chicken breasts on a cookie sheet and bake for 12–15 minutes.

Pepper Chicken

1	tsp. red pepper
1	tsp. paprika
$^1/_2$	tsp. black pepper
$^1/_4$	tsp. white pepper
1	tsp. salt
1	tsp. basil
2	whole chicken breasts, halved and boned, not skinned
2	cloves garlic, crushed
1	Tbsp. butter or margarine

Mix all dry ingredients in shallow bowl. Roll chicken in spice mixture, thoroughly coating all pieces. Place chicken pieces, skin side down, in a baking dish, trying not to let them touch one another. Sprinkle garlic evenly over chicken. Dot each piece with butter or margarine. Bake, uncovered, 30 minutes at 375°.

Spice mixture can be prepared any time. Store in large quantities to use as Cajun recipe seasoning.

Potato Cassoulet

3 slices bacon, diced
½ lb. Polish sausage, cut in chunks
6 chicken parts (preferably breasts)
½ cup dry white wine or water
1 16 oz. can whole tomatoes
1 15 oz. can pinto beans
3 medium potatoes (about one pound),
  peeled and halved
2 carrots, peeled and sliced
1 onion, halved and stuck with
  3 whole cloves
1 stalk celery, sliced
1 Tbsp. chopped parsley
½ cup bread crumbs

Easy

Serves 6–8
May prepare ahead
Preparation time:
  15 minutes
Bake 1 hour

Freezes well

Fry bacon in Dutch oven. Brown sausage and chicken parts lightly in bacon drippings; remove. Pour off fat. Boil wine in pan 2–3 minutes. Pour in tomatoes, beans, vegetables and seasonings. Boil, then cover and bake at 375° for 40 minutes. Sprinkle bread crumbs on top. Bake 15–20 minutes more, uncovered, until crumbs are brown.

Poulet Louisian

Easy

Serves 4
Preparation time:
 30 minutes
Cook 20 minutes

1   frying chicken, cut up
Freshly ground pepper
1/3   cup flour
2   Tbsp. olive oil or Crisco®
1/4   green pepper, sliced thinly
1   onion, sliced thinly
2   garlic cloves, crushed, or 1/4 tsp. garlic salt
1/2   bay leaf
1   tsp. dried parsley
1/4   tsp. dried thyme
3   oz. tomato paste
1/2   cup chicken broth or 1/2 cup water
    and 1 bouillon cube
1/2   cup red burgundy

Season chicken pieces with fresh pepper. Flour lightly (in small bag), then brown in oil or shortening. Remove chicken as it browns and keep warm in 325° oven. Sauté onion and green pepper in remaining oil until limp. Add garlic, bay leaf, parsley and thyme and sauté 5 minutes. Stir in remaining ingredients and bring almost to a boil. Return chicken to pan, lower heat, cover and cook about 20 minutes until chicken is tender.

Rosemary Chicken
with Bell Peppers

1	large green bell pepper
1	large yellow bell pepper
1	large tomato
12	cloves garlic, peeled
2	tsp. rosemary, crushed
2	tsp. grated lemon rind
3	Tbsp. olive oil
$^1\!/_2$	tsp. salt
$^1\!/_2$	tsp. black pepper
2	whole chicken breasts, split

Easy

Serves 4
Partially prepare
 ahead
Preparation time:
 10 minutes
Bake 1 hour

Cut peppers and tomato into large pieces, about 1" square. In a large bowl, mix peppers, tomato, garlic cloves, 1 tsp. rosemary, 1 tsp. lemon rind, 2 Tbsp. olive oil, salt and pepper. (Can be prepared to this point and refrigerated, if desired.) Rub chicken with remaining rosemary, lemon rind and oil. Place chicken in heavy casserole dish or Dutch oven; pour pepper mixture over chicken. Bake, covered, 45 minutes at 375°. Uncover; bake another 15 minutes to let excess moisture cook off.

Sautéed Chicken and Mushrooms

Easy

Serves 6–8
Preparation time:
 5 minutes
Cook 10–15 minutes

A simple, yet elegant dish!

8   boned, skinless chicken breasts, halved
2–3 Tbsp.butter
$^1/_2$ lb. fresh mushrooms
$^1/_3$ cup Madeira wine or sherry
$^1/_2$ cup cream
Pinch salt and pepper
Parsley, chopped

Pound chicken breasts until $^1/_2$ inch or less in thickness. In large skillet, brown chicken breasts in butter. Midway through browning, add mushrooms and sauté with chicken. When chicken is browned, add wine and simmer 2 minutes, then add cream. Cook until thick. Add salt and pepper. Remove chicken breasts to a platter and pour mushroom mixture over them. Sprinkle with parsley. Serve immediately.

Tarragon Chicken

1 frying or roasting chicken, cut up
$\frac{1}{4}$ cup soy sauce
$\frac{1}{4}$ cup tarragon vinegar
2 Tbsp. olive oil
1–2 bay leaves
Pepper
1–2 cloves garlic, minced
Sprinkle of tarragon (optional)

Preheat oven to 350°. Place chicken pieces in 9x12 baking dish. Mix together all other ingredients and pour over chicken. Bake, covered, 30 minutes. Uncover, bake 30 minutes longer.

Easy

Serves 4
Preparation time:
5 minutes
Bake 1 hour

Brandied Cornish Hens

Moderate

Serves 2
Preparation time:
15 minutes
Roast 1 hour

Can also be pre-
pared on grill

2	rock cornish game hens
$\frac{1}{2}$	cup fresh parsley, minced
$\frac{1}{2}$	tsp. tarragon
$\frac{1}{2}$	tsp. salt
$\frac{1}{2}$	cup butter, softened
$\frac{1}{2}$	cup currant jelly
$\frac{1}{2}$	cup brandy

Remove giblets and rinse hens in cold water; pat dry. Mix herbs, salt, $\frac{1}{4}$ cup butter. Put half of butter mixture in each hen and skewer closed. Rub hens with remaining butter and place in shallow roasting pan. Roast at 375° for 30 minutes. Heat jelly and brandy until jelly melts. Pour over hens and roast 30 minutes longer, basting every 10 minutes with brandy mixture. Remove from pan and serve with wild rice.

Quail à la Campagne

6 quail
6 Tbsp. butter
3 Tbsp. flour
2 cups chicken broth
$\frac{1}{2}$ cup dry sherry
Salt and pepper to taste

Brown quail in butter in a heavy skillet. Remove to baking dish. Add flour to butter in skillet and stir well to make a roux. Slowly add chicken broth, sherry, salt and pepper. Blend well and pour over quail. Cover and bake at 350° for 1 hour.

Easy

Serves 6
May prepare ahead
Preparation time:
15 minutes
Bake 1 hour

Serve with wild rice

Seafood

Baked Orange Roughy with Dijon Sauce

Fish:
6   orange roughy fillets
Salt and freshly ground pepper
$^1/_4$ cup butter
1   cup crushed almonds
Lemon slices

Easy

Serves 6
Partially prepare
 ahead
Preparation time:
 30 minutes
Bake 20 minutes

Dijon sauce:
2   Tbsp. butter
$^1/_2$ cup sliced green onion
3   Tbsp. Dijon mustard
$^1/_4$ cup white wine
1   cup sour cream
Freshly ground pepper to taste

Fish:
Preheat oven to 350°. Dip fillets in melted butter and season to taste with salt and freshly ground pepper. Place in buttered baking dish. Sprinkle almonds over fillets. Bake until flaky, approximately 20 minutes.

Dijon sauce:
Sauté onions in butter until tender. Add mustard and wine, stir until well blended. Stir in sour cream until heated, do not boil. (Dijon sauce may be prepared several hours ahead. Refrigerate and reheat slowly, being careful not to boil.) Pour over fillets, garnish with lemon slices.

Cheesy Broiled Flounder

Easy

Serves 4–6
Preparation time:
 10 minutes
Broil 5 minutes

2   lb. flounder or any mild whitefish
    fillets
2   Tbsp. lemon juice
$^1/_2$ cup freshly grated Parmesan cheese
$^1/_4$ cup softened butter
3   Tbsp. mayonnaise
3   green onions, chopped
$^1/_4$ tsp. salt
Dash hot sauce

Place fillets in single layer on greased broiler rack. Brush with lemon juice. Combine cheese, butter, mayonnaise, green onions, salt and hot sauce. Broil fillets 4 to 6 minutes. Spread with cheese mixture. Broil 30 seconds longer or until browned and bubbly.

Flounder Fillets with Tomato and Olives

1 medium onion, chopped
3 large tomatoes, peeled, seeded and chopped
4 servings of flounder or sole (¹/₄ lb. each)
8 black olives, sliced
4 Tbsp. unsalted butter
¹/₂ tsp. paprika
³/₄ tsp. salt
1 Tbsp. lemon juice
1 Tbsp. minced parsley

Easy

Serves 4
Preparation time:
 15 minutes
Bake 25 minutes

Cook onion and 2 Tbsp. butter in skillet over low heat. When onion is soft add tomato, ¹/₄ tsp. paprika, ¹/₂ tsp. salt, 1 Tbsp. lemon juice and 1¹/₂ tsp. minced parsley. Simmer until mixture is thick and not overly juicy. Stir in remaining butter and add more lemon juice and salt to taste. Sprinkle fish with ¹/₄ tsp. salt and ¹/₄ tsp. paprika and fold in half. Pour tomato mixture into baking dish and arrange fish on top. Sprinkle with olives and bake at 350° for 25 minutes. Top with 1¹/₂ tsp. minced parsley.

Grilled Salmon
with Fresh Herb Butter

Easy

Serves 6
Preparation time:
 10 minutes
Grill 10 minutes

Fish:
6   salmon steaks or fillets (6 oz. each)
3   Tbsp. soy sauce
3   Tbsp. fresh lemon juice
Olive oil

Herb butter:
2   sticks lightly salted butter, melted
2–3 Tbsp. chopped fresh, basil, tarragon or
    dill

Fish:
Rinse salmon under cold water and pat dry. Coat the fish lightly with olive oil to prevent sticking on the grill. Combine soy sauce and lemon juice, sprinkle over the fish. (Before lighting the grill, spray metal grate with a vegetable oil spray to prevent sticking.) When grill is very hot, place steaks (if fillets, skin side down) on the grill and cover with lid. Cook 5 to 10 minutes (firm to the touch). If using fillets, skin will stick to the grill. Remove fish leaving skin on the grill (skin can be removed later with a metal spatula).

Herb butter:
Combine butter and herbs; serve with fish.

Grilled Swordfish

12 Tbsp. butter ($^3/_4$ cup)
2 lb. swordfish or snapper
Salt and pepper to taste
3 lemons, juiced
1 Tbsp. peppercorns
1 lemon, sliced
1 clove garlic, minced
3 Tbsp. minced parsley

Easy

Serves 4
Preparation time:
 5 minutes
Grill 20 minutes

Dot 6 Tbsp. of butter on bottom of foil pan. Place fish on top of butter. Salt and pepper to taste. Squeeze lemons on top of fish. Top with 6 Tbsp. butter slices. Press peppercorns onto fish. Top with lemon slices, garlic and parsley. Cook 20 minutes on medium heat, cover grill, do not turn fish.

Grilled Swordfish Steaks with Avocado Butter

Easy

Serves 4
Partially prepare
* ahead*
Preparation time:
* 20 minutes*
Marinate 1–4 hours
Grill 10 minutes

$\frac{1}{2}$ cup soy sauce
1   tsp. lemon zest
$\frac{1}{4}$ cup fresh lemon juice
2   cloves garlic, crushed
2   tsp. Dijon mustard
$\frac{1}{2}$ cup Crisco® oil
4   6 oz. swordfish steaks
2   lemons cut into wedges
Parsley, chopped

Avocado butter:
$\frac{1}{2}$ cup butter
$\frac{1}{2}$ cup avocado
5   Tbsp. lemon juice
2   Tbsp. parsley
2   cloves garlic

Combine soy sauce, lemon zest, lemon juice, garlic, mustard and oil in food processor and blend. Pierce fish with a fork and pour marinade over fish. Marinate for 1-4 hours. Grill fish for 5 minutes on each side.

Avocado butter:
Combine butter, avocado, lemon juice, parsley and garlic in food processor and blend. Roll up in parchment paper to make a log. Freeze until needed. Serve swordfish with a medallion of avocado butter. Garnish with lemon wedges and parsley.

Hot Tuna Sandwiches

3   Tbsp. mayonnaise
1   6 oz. can tuna (drained)
1½ cups (½ lb.) cheddar cheese, shredded
½   cup chili sauce
¼   cup onion, chopped
1   4 oz. jar diced pimientos, drained
12 stuffed olives, chopped (optional)
2   hard boiled eggs, chopped (optional)
10 hot dog buns (hamburger buns may be
    substituted)

Combine all ingredients and mix well. Divide mixture among buns. Wrap each sandwich separately in foil. Bake 15–20 minutes at 375°.

Easy

Serves 10
Preparation time:
 15 minutes
Bake 15–20 minutes

Freezes well

Marinated Halibut Steaks

Easy

Serves 4–6
Preparation time:
 5 minutes
Marinate 2 hours
Grill 10 minutes

2   lb. halibut steaks or any firm fish
³/₄   cup Crisco® oil or olive oil
1   medium onion, chopped
¹/₄   cup lemon juice (fresh, frozen or bottled)
¹/₄   cup Dijon-style mustard
1   Tbsp. fresh dill, chopped
2–3 cloves garlic, minced
Fresh ground pepper

Place fish in a flat glass baking pan. Combine other ingredients in a small bowl. Pour over fish, cover and refrigerate for two hours. Drain and grill, basting with the marinade, about 8–10 minutes or until fish tests done (flaky).

Oriental Tuna Steaks

Easy

Serves 6
Partially prepare
 ahead
Preparation time:
 10 minutes
Marinate at least
 5 hours
Broil 10 minutes

This marinade may
be used with other
firm fish

3   Tbsp. chopped fresh ginger
2   large garlic cloves, pressed
1   tsp. brown sugar
¹/₂   cup rice wine (may substitute sherry)
¹/₄   tsp. hot chili oil
¹/₂   cup Crisco® oil
6   tuna steaks, ¹/₂" to 1" thick

In a shallow non-metal pan combine first 6 ingredients and mix well. Marinate tuna steaks (covered with plastic wrap) for 5 hours or more. Prepare either charcoal grill or broiler pan. To grill, cook 5-6 minutes per side over medium heat until fish flakes. To broil, cook 5-6 minutes per side, until fish flakes.

Salmon en Papillote

Moderate

Serves 6
*Partially prepare
  ahead*
*Preparation time:
  20 minutes*
Bake 8 minutes

2 lb. salmon fillets, cut into
  6 serving pieces
5 carrots, julienned
³/₄ lb. sliced mushrooms
6 Tbsp. butter, melted
Juice from 1 lemon
First two inches of 1 leek
Salt and pepper to taste
4 Tbsp. dill
6 Tbsp. shallots
6 Tbsp. vermouth or dry white wine

Preheat oven to 500°. Cut fillets into 6 serving pieces. Cut 6 sheets of aluminum foil or parchment into 12 rounds. Sauté mushrooms in 2 Tbsp. of butter. Add lemon juice and cook one minute. Add carrots and leek, cook 7–8 minutes. Sprinkle with dill and set aside. Brush rounds with remaining melted butter. Place vegetable mixture on rounds. Lay fish over vegetables. Sprinkle with shallots and 1 Tbsp. of wine. Salt and pepper to taste. Crimp edges, this will expand. (May be prepared ahead to this point.) Bake for 8 minutes.

Sole Meunière

Moderate

Serves 2
Preparation time:
 12 minutes
Cook 5 minutes

Orange roughy or
red snapper may be
substituted.

2   Dover sole fillets
Salt and pepper to taste
Flour for dredging
3-4 Tbsp. clarified butter

Sauce:
2-3 Tbsp. butter
1-2 Tbsp. capers (bottled in good wine and
      vinegar)

Preheat pan on medium high. Dry excess moisture from fish. Score skin side of fish. Dredge with flour, salt and pepper. Sauté over high heat in clarified butter 2 minutes on each side. Remove to hot platter.

Sauce:
Melt butter, add capers. When sizzling, pour over fish.

Swordfish with Mustard Sauce

¼ cup white wine
3 Tbsp. minced shallots
¼ cup whipping cream
1 cup chilled unsalted butter, cut into small pieces
¼ cup fresh lemon juice
2 Tbsp. mustard
Salt and white pepper to taste
4 swordfish steaks
3 Tbsp. olive oil
3 Tbsp. parsley, basil and tarragon

Moderate

Serves 4
Preparation time:
 12 minutes
Grill 10 minutes

Boil wine and shallots until liquid is reduced to 3 Tbsp. Add cream and boil until it is reduced by half. Remove from heat and whisk in butter 1 Tbsp. at a time. Whisk in lemon juice, mustard, salt and pepper. Keep sauce warm. Drizzle oil on swordfish and sprinkle with herbs. Grill fish 4-5 minutes per side. Divide sauce among plates and top with fish. Garnish with lemon and parsley.

Tuna with Salsa

Easy

Serves 6
May prepare ahead
Preparation time:
 10 minutes

Freezes well

When it's too hot to cook, serve this for a light, easy meal.

3   large, ripe tomatoes
1   medium purple onion
¼   cup fresh cilantro
3   fresh jalapeno peppers,
     seeds and membranes removed
2   large cans tuna
Saltine crackers

Chop tomatoes; drain off excess liquid and place in medium bowl. In food processor, chop onion with cilantro; add to tomatoes. Chop jalapenos in food processor; add to tomato mixture. Chill if desired. Serve salsa and tuna in separate bowls. To eat, heap tuna on crackers; spoon salsa over all.

Jambalaya

2 Tbsp. unsalted butter
1¹/₂ cups chopped Andouille or Kielbasa
       sausage
1¹/₂ cups chopped onions
1 cup celery
1 cup chopped green pepper
1 cup chopped chicken
4 cloves garlic, minced
4 medium tomatoes, peeled and chopped
¹/₂ cup tomato sauce

¹/₂ cup green onions
2 bay leaves
1 tsp. cayenne pepper
1 tsp. black pepper
1 tsp. white pepper
2 tsp. oregano leaves
2 tsp. basil
2 tsp. thyme
6 cups cooked rice
2 dozen shrimp
2 dozen oysters

Moderate

Serves 8
May prepare ahead
Preparation time:
 20 minutes
Cook 30 minutes

Great for main
course

In a 4 quart pan, melt butter and cook sausage. Add onion, celery, green pepper and sauté until tender. Add chicken, garlic, tomatoes, tomato sauce, green onions, seasonings and cook until chicken is tender. Simmer on very low heat for 30 minutes. The flavors will be enhanced if made the day before. Add all the above to rice. Cook for 20-30 minutes until warm. Add shrimp and oysters and cook until shrimp is done (about 10 minutes). Watch closely so that seafood is not overcooked.

Seafood in Pastry Shells

Easy

Serves 6–8
Preparation time:
20 minutes
Cook 20 minutes

2 Tbsp. unsalted butter
1½ lb. shrimp, shelled
2 Tbsp. unsalted butter
1½ lb. bay scallops
½ cup heavy cream
¼ tsp. arrowroot or corn starch
2 tsp. tarragon
Fresh lemon juice to taste
⅛ tsp. cayenne pepper
Baked pie crust or patty shells

Heat 2 Tbsp. butter in large skillet. Sauté shrimp until done. Remove shrimp with slotted spoon. Add remaining 2 Tbsp. butter. Sauté scallops until done. Remove with slotted spoon. Add cream, arrowroot, tarragon and lemon juice. Simmer until slightly thick. Add shrimp and scallops. Simmer until heated through. Pour in warm pie shell or warm patty shells.

Seafood Marinade

Easy

Yield: ³/₄ cup
Prepare ahead
Preparation time:
15 minutes

¼ cup olive oil
½ cup dry white wine
1 tsp. dry chervil
1 tsp. paprika
Salt to taste

Blend all together. Marinate 2 lb. scallops, shrimp or lobster tails for 2 hours.

Seafood Sauce

1 envelope whipped topping mix
¼ cup horseradish
1½ tsp. salt
⅛ tsp. paprika
Dash of cayenne pepper
½ tsp. lemon juice
2 Tbsp. milk

Prepare envelope of whipped topping mix omitting the vanilla. Stir in remaining ingredients. Serve over grilled or broiled seafood.

Easy

Yield: 2 cups
May prepare ahead
Preparation time:
20 minutes

Baked Shrimp Oregano

1 lb. raw shrimp, shelled and deveined
2 Tbsp. lemon juice
½ cup butter or margarine, melted
½ cup dry bread crumbs
2 cloves garlic, crushed
2 Tbsp. chopped parsley
2 Tbsp. Parmesan cheese
1 tsp. oregano leaves
Lemon wedges

Preheat oven to 350°. Wash shrimp, drain well. Arrange shrimp in 8x10 shallow baking dish; sprinkle with lemon juice. Combine butter, crumbs, garlic, parsley, Parmesan and oregano. Mix well, spread over shrimp. Bake, uncovered, 15 minutes, then broil until crumbs are browned, approximately 3 minutes. Garnish with lemon wedges.

Easy

Serves 4
Preparation time:
10 minutes
Bake 18 minutes

Easy and delicious

Barbecued Shrimp

2   dozen large shrimp

Marinade:
$^1/_2$ stick unsalted butter, melted
       or $^1/_2$ cup olive oil
4   garlic cloves, minced
1   tsp. cayenne pepper
1   tsp. black pepper
$^1/_2$ tsp. crushed red pepper
1   tsp. thyme leaves
1   tsp. rosemary leaves
1   tsp. oregano leaves
Juice of 1 lemon

Combine butter or olive oil with garlic, both types of pepper, red pepper, thyme, rosemary, oregano and lemon juice. Marinate shrimp for 1 hour. Grill shrimp 1 minute or less per side. Warm marinade and serve in bowls with shrimp and French bread on the side. Garnish with lemon wedges.

Bay Scallops with Mushrooms

Fish stock:
$1^1/_2$ cups water
$^1/_2$ lb. cod
2   bay leaves
$^1/_2$ cup carrots, sliced
$^1/_4$ cup onion, chopped

¹/₄ tsp. celery salt
¹/₄ tsp. rosemary

Scallops:
4   Tbsp. butter
³/₄ lb. bay scallops
²/₃ cup sliced mushrooms
3   Tbsp. flour
1¹/₄ cups fish stock
¹/₄ cup dry white wine
Salt and pepper to taste
10   oz. hot, cooked linguine
2   scallions, finely chopped
¹/₈ tsp. nutmeg
4   sprigs parsley

Fish stock:
In medium saucepan, cook all ingredients over medium heat for 20–25 minutes. Fish will be flaky. Strain; use strained liquid in scallops recipe.

Scallops:
Heat butter in medium skillet. Add scallops and mushrooms; sauté over moderately high heat for 2–3 minutes. Add flour; stir in fish stock and wine. Cook, stirring, until mixture boils and thickens. Add salt and pepper to taste.

Warm four plates; place a serving of linguine on each plate. Spoon scallops over linguine. Sprinkle with scallions and nutmeg. Garnish with parsley.

Broiled Scallops

Easy

Serves 4
Partially prepare
  ahead
Preparation time:
  15 minutes
Broil 5 to 10 minutes

Super easy

2   lb. sea scallops
$1/4$ cup melted butter
3   Tbsp. Italian style bread crumbs
$1/8$ tsp. garlic salt
$1/8$ tsp. dry mustard
$1/2$ tsp. paprika
2   Tbsp. sherry
Lemon slices

Rinse scallops and pat dry. Pour melted butter into broiler pan. Add scallops and coat with butter. Combine dry ingredients and sprinkle over scallops. May be prepared a couple of hours before broiling. Refrigerate until ready to broil; you may need to increase cooking time. Broil and brown 5 to 7 minutes. Turn off broiler and let scallops heat 3 to 5 minutes longer. Sprinkle scallops with sherry and serve immediately with lemon slices.

Chicken and Scampi

3½ lb. chicken pieces (breasts and thighs)
1   Tbsp. salt
½   tsp. pepper
¼   cup butter
3   small onions, chopped
1   clove garlic, minced
3   Tbsp. snipped parsley
½   cup port wine
8   oz. can tomato sauce
1   tsp. dried basil
1   lb. shelled shrimp
Snipped parsley for garnish

Moderate

Serves 6
Partially prepare
 ahead
Preparation time:
 1 hour
Cook 45 minutes

Serve with rice.

Rub chicken with salt and pepper. In a large skillet, sauté chicken in butter until golden on all sides. Add onion, garlic, parsley, wine, tomato sauce, and basil. Simmer covered about 30 minutes until chicken is tender. (Can be prepared ahead to this point.) Push chicken aside; add shrimp. Cook uncovered until shrimp is pink. Place chicken pieces in serving dish; top with shrimp. Pour sauce over and garnish with parsley. If necessary, skim fat from surface of sauce.

Maryland Crab Imperial

Easy

Serves 4
Partially prepare
 ahead
Preparation time:
 10 minutes
Cooking time:
20 minutes

Serve in pastry shell

1 lb. backfin crabmeat
  (do not substitute canned)
$^1/_8$ tsp. pepper
$^1/_2$ tsp. salt
1 egg, slightly beaten
$^1/_3$ cup mayonnaise
1 tsp. prepared yellow mustard
1 whole pimiento, chopped
Mayonnaise and paprika for topping

Combine mayonnaise, salt, pepper, mustard, egg and pimiento. Blend with fork. Gently fold in crabmeat which has been picked over for shell, being careful not to disturb lumps. (Can be mixed a few hours ahead.) Heap into shells. Top with a light coating of mayonnaise and sprinkle with paprika. Bake at 350° for 20 minutes or until bubbly and slightly browned.

North Carolina Crab Cakes

Crab cakes:

1	lb. crabmeat (preferably fresh)
2	medium eggs
$1/_2$	cup finely minced green pepper
$1/_2$	cup finely minced celery
4	Tbsp. finely minced onion
1	Tbsp. chopped fresh parsley
1	Tbsp. baking powder
1	Tbsp. Worcestershire sauce
1	Tbsp. mayonnaise
2	slices fresh bread, cubed
2-3	Tbsp. Crisco® oil

Cocktail sauce:

6	Tbsp. chili sauce
1	tsp. Worcestershire sauce
2	ripe tomatoes, seeded, peeled and chopped
1	tsp. prepared horseradish
1	Tbsp. chopped fresh parsley

Crab cakes:

Mix all ingredients well and lightly form patties. Place in refrigerator to chill slightly. Heat oil in large skillet and sauté crab cakes until golden brown on each side. Serve immediately with homemade cocktail sauce.

Cocktail sauce:

Combine all ingredients and chill.

Moderate

Serves 4–6
Partially prepare
* ahead*
Preparation time:
* 30 minutes*
Cook 4 minutes

Especially good
with fresh blue crab

Oyster Lovers' Delight

Easy

Serves 2
Cook 10 minutes

Serve with a green salad and a glass of dry white wine

2   Tbsp. butter
2   Tbsp. flour
1   pint oysters; reserve oyster liquor and add chicken stock to make one cup
$^1/_2$ tsp. salt
$^1/_4$ tsp. paprika
$^3/_4$ tsp. curry powder
Buttered toast squares
1   tsp. lemon juice
Chopped parsley

Melt butter in 10 inch skillet. Whisk in flour. Slowly stir in oyster liquor and chicken stock. Add salt, paprika and curry powder. When smooth and hot, prepare toast and add oysters to mixture. Heat but do not boil. Add lemon juice. Pour over buttered toast and sprinkle with parsley.

Shrimp Creole

1½ lb. shrimp, fresh or frozen,
   shelled and deveined
¼ cup chopped onion
¼ cup green pepper
1 clove garlic, finely chopped
¼ cup melted butter
3 Tbsp. flour
1 tsp. chili powder
1 tsp. salt
Pepper to taste
2 cups canned tomatoes

Peel shrimp and clean; if large cut in half. In a large skillet, cook onion, green pepper and garlic in butter until tender. Blend in flour and seasonings. Add tomatoes and cook until thick, stirring constantly. Add uncooked shrimp. Simmer uncovered for about 20 minutes. Serve in a rice ring.

Moderate

Serves 4–6
May prepare ahead
Preparation time:
   20 minutes
Cook 20 minutes

Freezes well

For extra zing, add cayenne pepper, white pepper, oregano, paprika to taste

Shrimp Elegante

Moderate

Serves 8
May prepare ahead
Preparation time:
  10 minutes
Marinate 4–5 hours
Broil 5 minutes

3   lb. shrimp, peeled
$^1/_2$ cup butter
$^3/_4$ cup olive oil
2   cups chopped onion
3   cloves garlic
$^1/_4$ cup chopped parsley
1   tsp. oregano
$^1/_2$ cup white wine
$^1/_2$ cup Italian salad dressing
$^1/_4$ cup water
1   Tbsp. + 1 tsp. chicken bouillon granules
Freshly ground pepper to taste

Place shrimp in boiling water 30 seconds. Drain and place in shallow broiling pan. Combine butter and olive oil in medium saucepan. Heat until butter melts. Add onion, garlic, parsley, and oregano. Cook until onion is transparent, stirring occasionally. Add remaining ingredients, stirring until bouillon is dissolved. Reduce heat to low and simmer 5 minutes. Pour over shrimp; cover and marinate in refrigerator 4 to 5 hours. Uncover and broil 4" from heat 5 minutes or until done, being careful not to overcook. Serve shrimp over fettucine or rice. Pass the warm marinade.

Shrimp Puff

6	eggs, beaten
2	Tbsp. parsley
$\frac{1}{2}$	tsp. salt
2	cups tiny cooked shrimp
3	cups milk
$\frac{3}{4}$	tsp. dry mustard
2	cups shredded cheddar cheese
10	slices bread, crust removed, cubed

Easy

Serves 8
Partially prepare
  ahead
Preparation time:
  15 minutes
Refrigerate
  overnight
Bake 1 hour

Mix all ingredients except bread cubes. Add bread cubes; put in soufflé dish or $7\frac{1}{2}$x$11\frac{1}{2}$ dish. Let sit overnight in refrigerator. Bake uncovered at 325° for 1 hour or until center is set.

Spicy Barbequed Shrimp

5	lb. raw shrimp with peel on shrimp
1	onion, sliced
$1\frac{1}{2}$	cups butter, sliced
1	large bottle Italian dressing
Juice of 2 lemons	
6	Tbsp. black pepper

Easy

Serves 6
Preparation time:
  10 minutes
Bake 40 minutes

Serve with hot
French bread for
dunking in sauce

Remove heads from large shrimp; do not peel. Place shrimp in large shallow pan; top with onion slices; cover with butter slices. Add dressing and lemon juice; sprinkle with pepper. Bake in 400° oven for 40 minutes, turning gently every 10 minutes.

Vegetables and Side Dishes

Baked Corn

1   small onion, minced
2   Tbsp. butter or margarine
2   Tbsp. flour
2   Tbsp. brown sugar
1   tsp. salt (or to taste)
$\frac{1}{2}$ tsp. black pepper (or to taste)
$\frac{1}{2}$ tsp. nutmeg (or to taste)
1   cup milk
2   eggs, beaten
2   cups whole kernel corn (fresh off cob, if possible)

Easy

Serves 6–8
Preparation time:
 10 minutes
Bake 45 minutes

Good holiday recipe

In a small saucepan, cook onion in butter 5 minutes. Blend flour, sugar and seasoning. Add milk and cook, stirring until thickened. Gradually stir in eggs. Add corn and mix well. Bake in 9-inch pie pan at 325° for 45 minutes.

Brandied Cranberries

Easy

Serves 6–8
May prepare ahead
Cook 20 minutes

Freezes well

1½ cups sugar
1½ cups water
1 lb. fresh cranberries
¼ cup brandy
1½ tsp. cinnamon
1 tsp. ground cloves
Rind of 1 orange, chopped fine

Dissolve sugar and water in a 2-quart saucepan and bring to a boil. Add cranberries and cook 5 minutes longer, until the cranberries pop open. Remove from heat and add brandy, cinnamon, cloves, and orange rind. Mix well. Serve warm or cold.

Broccoli Soufflé I

Easy

Serves 4–6
May prepare ahead
Preparation time:
 15 minutes
Bake 20–30 minutes

2 10 oz. pkg. frozen broccoli florets
1 clove finely minced garlic
1 small onion, chopped
1 can cream of mushroom soup
4 oz. Alouette cheese (herb and garlic)

Cook broccoli according to package directions and drain; set aside. Sauté onions in butter. Mix all ingredients well and put in greased 1½ or 2 quart soufflé dish. Bake 20–30 minutes at 350° or until bubbly.

Broccoli Soufflé II

2   10 oz. pkg. chopped frozen broccoli
1   can cream of celery soup
1   cup mayonnaise
3   Tbsp. chopped onion
2   eggs, well beaten
1   cup grated cheddar cheese
1   stick melted butter
1   stack Ritz® crackers, crushed

Moderate

Serves 6–8
May prepare ahead
Preparation time:
30 minutes
Bake 1 hour

Cook, drain and cool broccoli. Mix the mayonnaise, onion, eggs and cheese and add to broccoli. Put mixture into greased 2 quart baking dish. Melt butter and add crushed crackers. Mix until crackers are moistened. Spread evenly across top of mixture. Bake 1 hour at 350°. Cool slightly before serving.

Buffet Carrots

Easy

Serves 6–8
Preparation time:
 20 minutes
Bake 15–20 minutes

2$^1/_2$ lb. carrots, cut into strips
$^1/_2$ cup mayonnaise
2 Tbsp. minced onion
1 Tbsp. horseradish
Dash salt and pepper
Paprika for garnish

Cook carrots until just tender. Drain liquid, saving 2 tablespoons. Arrange carrots in casserole dish. Combine liquid from carrots, mayonnaise, onions and horseradish. Season carrots to taste with salt and pepper. Pour sauce over carrots, sprinkle with paprika. Bake 15–20 minutes at 375°.

Cauliflower with Caper Sauce

Easy

Serves 6
Preparation time:
 10 minutes
Cook 15 minutes

1 whole large cauliflower, cut into florets
1 Tbsp. cornstarch
1 cup milk
3 Tbsp. butter
3 Tbsp. lemon juice
1 Tbsp. grated onion
1 tsp. turmeric
Pepper to taste
3–4 Tbsp. capers, drained

Cook cauliflower until tender. Keep warm. Blend cornstarch and milk. Add the butter, lemon juice, grated onion, turmeric, and pepper. Stir until sauce thickens. Fold in capers. Pour over cauliflower.

Cheese-Topped Green Beans

1 lb. green beans in 1" pieces
¼ cup dry onion soup mix
1 cup water
3 Tbsp. melted butter
⅓ cup toasted slivered almonds
3 Tbsp. grated Parmesan cheese
½ tsp. paprika

Easy

Serves 4–6
Preparation time:
 5 minutes
Cook 30 minutes

Combine green beans, onion soup mix and water. Cover and cook over low heat 20–30 minutes. Drain and spoon into serving dish. Add butter, almonds, cheese and toss lightly. Sprinkle with paprika.

Chilies Rellenos

Moderate

Serves 8
Preparation time:
 15 minutes
Cook 45 minutes

Add bacon or ham
for a "meatier" dish

5   4 oz. cans green chilies, chopped
³/₄ lb. grated cheddar cheese
³/₄ lb. grated Monterey Jack cheese
4   eggs, separated
1   12 oz. can evaporated milk
2   Tbsp. flour
Salt and pepper to taste
1   15 oz. can tomato sauce (optional)
Hot sauce

Cover bottom of 9x13 greased pan with ¹/₂ the chilies. Sprinkle ¹/₂ the cheddar cheese, then ¹/₂ the Monterey Jack, over the chilies. Repeat the layers. Beat the egg yolks. Add evaporated milk, flour, salt and pepper. Stiffly beat egg whites and gently fold into yolk mixture. Pour egg mixture over chilies and cheese. Bake at 350° for 45 minutes. If desired, pour tomato sauce over all before the last 10 minutes of cooking time. Serve with hot sauce.

Corn Fritters

Easy

Yield: 16 fritters
Partially prepare
 ahead
Preparation time:
 10 minutes
Fry 20 minutes

1   cup unsifted all purpose flour
1   tsp. baking powder
1   tsp. salt
²/₃ cup milk
1   tsp. Crisco® oil
1   cup cooked whole kernel corn

Mix flour, baking powder and salt. Add milk and oil. Beat with rotary beater until smooth. Stir in corn. Drop by large tablespoons into hot deep oil (360°). Serve with maple syrup.

Your kids are sure to love these!

Corn Pudding

2 cups frozen corn, thawed and drained
4 Tbsp. flour
2 tsp. sugar
1 tsp. salt
2 well beaten eggs
1 Tbsp. melted butter
2 cups whole milk
Brown sugar (optional)

Easy

Serves 4
May prepare ahead
Preparation time:
  10 minutes
Bake 1 hour

Mix together the corn, flour, sugar and salt. Combine eggs, melted butter and milk. Add to corn mixture and pour into greased baking dish. Bake at 350° for 1 hour. Stir from bottom 2–3 times during first half hour of baking so the pudding will set properly. You may sprinkle the top with brown sugar and put under the broiler before serving.

Creamy Lemon Spinach

Easy

Serves 6
Preparation time:
 20 minutes
Bake 30 minutes

3   10 oz. pkg. chopped frozen spinach
3   3 oz. pkg. cream cheese
3   Tbsp. butter, softened
3   tsp. grated lemon rind
3   tsp. lemon juice
6   Tbsp. seasoned dry bread crumbs
3   Tbsp. butter, melted
Lemon rind strips

Cook spinach according to package directions; drain well. Combine next four ingredients; mix well. Stir in spinach. Spoon mixture into a lightly greased 6-cup casserole. Combine bread crumbs and melted butter and mix well and spoon over spinach. Bake uncovered at 350° for 30 minutes. Garnish with lemon rind.

Fried Zucchini

Easy

Serves 4
Preparation time:
 10 minutes
Cook 20 minutes

3   medium zucchini
$\frac{1}{4}$ cup olive oil
2   Tbsp. vinegar
$\frac{1}{4}$ tsp. oregano
$\frac{1}{2}$ tsp. basil
$\frac{1}{2}$ tsp. salt
3   Tbsp. grated Parmesan cheese

Slice zucchini, leaving skins on. Place in skillet with olive oil, vinegar, oregano, basil and salt. Simmer for 8 to 10 minutes. Turn zucchini carefully with spatula. Sprinkle with parmesan cheese. Cover and simmer for 10 additional minutes or until tender.

Gingered Broccoli

1   bunch fresh broccoli
1   tsp. shaved fresh ginger root
1   Tbsp. butter

Easy

*Serves 6
Cooking time:
   20 minutes*

Cook broccoli until crisp-tender. Shave ginger root and add butter; melt. Toss with broccoli and serve.

Green Beans

Moderate

Serves 8
Preparation time:
 30 minutes
Cook 15 minutes

6	slices bacon
3/4	cup chopped onions
1/2	cup green pepper
2	Tbsp. flour
2	Tbsp. brown sugar
1	Tbsp. Worcestershire sauce
1/2	tsp. salt
1/4	tsp. pepper
1/8	tsp. dry mustard
1	16 oz. can peeled tomatoes
1	16 oz. can green beans, drained

Sauté bacon until crisp. Remove from skillet. Remove all but 3 Tbsp. drippings. Add onions and green pepper to pan. Sauté until tender. Blend in flour, sugar, Worcestershire, salt, pepper and mustard. Cut up tomatoes and add to skillet. Stir until thick. Add green beans and heat through. Place in serving dish and top with bacon.

Ham It Up with Potatoes

4   large russet or red skinned potatoes
4   Tbsp. butter
1   egg, slightly beaten
White pepper to taste
Salt to taste
$^1/_3$ cup milk
$^1/_4$ cup Parmesan cheese
$^1/_4$ lb. boiled or baked ham, sliced
$^1/_2$ lb. sliced mozzarella cheese
Bread crumbs

Moderate

Serves 4
Partially prepare
  ahead
Preparation time:
  45 minutes
Bake 30 minutes

Boil potatoes with skins on, until tender, drain, and peel while hot. Mash through potato ricer into large bowl. Add butter, egg, white pepper, salt, milk and Parmesan cheese. Blend at medium to high speed with electric mixer until they become the consistency of mashed potatoes. Cut ham and mozzarella slices in quarters. Spread potato layer in lightly greased 1 quart deep casserole dish. Layer with part of ham and cheese. Repeat this process ending with a potato layer on top. Dot with butter. Sprinkle with bread crumbs. Bake 30 minutes at 350°.

Holiday Sweet Potato Casserole

Easy

Serves 8
May prepare ahead
Preparation time:
15 minutes
Bake 30 minutes

3 cups mashed sweet potatoes (may use canned)
1 cup sugar
1/2 cup melted butter
2 eggs, well beaten
1 tsp. vanilla
1/3 cup milk

Topping:
1/2 cup firmly packed brown sugar
1/4 cup all purpose flour
2 1/2 Tbsp. melted butter
1/2 cup chopped pecans

Combine potatoes, sugar, butter, eggs, vanilla and milk. Mix well. Spoon into a two quart casserole dish. Combine all of the topping ingredients, mixing well. Sprinkle over top of potato mixture before baking. Bake at 350° for 25–30 minutes.

Honeyed Carrots

Easy

Serves 6
Cook 20 minutes

3 cups sliced carrots
1/4 cup butter
2 tsp. cornstarch
1/3 cup honey
1/4 tsp. salt
1 tsp. lemon juice
1/8 tsp. cinnamon (or more to taste)

Boil carrots until tender and drain. Meanwhile: Melt butter, blend in cornstarch. Stir until there are no lumps. Add honey, salt, lemon juice and cinnamon. Cook, stirring constantly for 2–3 minutes or until thickened and clear. When carrots are done, add sauce to carrots and cook over low heat to mix.

Hot Tomatoes

4	large firm ripe tomatoes
$\frac{1}{4}$	cup flour
$\frac{1}{2}$	tsp. salt
$\frac{1}{2}$	tsp. dry mustard
$\frac{1}{4}$	tsp. paprika
1	Tbsp. finely chopped green onions
1	Tbsp. finely chopped green bell pepper
1	tsp. Worcestershire sauce
4	strips lean bacon, cut in half, partially cooked
$\frac{1}{2}$	cup grated sharp cheddar cheese

Easy

Serves 8
Preparation time:
 15 minutes
Cook 25–30 minutes

Preheat oven to 350°. Wash tomatoes and cut in half. Arrange, cut side up, in shallow baking dish. Combine next 7 ingredients. Spread equal portions of mixture on each tomato half. Lay 1 strip of bacon on each tomato. Sprinkle with grated cheese. Bake for 25 to 30 minutes.

Mushrooms Supreme

Easy

Serves 6
Partially prepare
  ahead
Preparation time:
  10–15 minutes
Bake 35 minutes

Great side dish with
grilled steak.

¹/₂ cup butter
¹/₄ cup sherry
1¹/₂ lb. fresh mushrooms, sliced
2 Tbsp. onion, minced
2 Tbsp. flour
1 cup sour cream
¹/₄ cup cream
¹/₂ tsp. salt
Pepper to taste (optional)
¹/₄ tsp. nutmeg
2 Tbsp. chopped fresh parsley
¹/₂ cup soft bread crumbs tossed in ¹/₂ cup melted butter.

Melt butter and sherry in heavy skillet. Add mushrooms and sauté until browned slightly and liquid is evaporated. Add onion and sauté until soft. Stir in flour; cook 5 minutes over low heat, stirring constantly. Blend in sour cream and cream. Add salt, pepper, nutmeg; cook until thickened. Stir in parsley. Pour into buttered casserole and sprinkle with bread crumbs. Bake in oven at 325° for 35 minutes or until lightly browned.

Onion Jam

¼ cup butter
2 tsp. Crisco® oil
8 large Bermuda onions, thinly sliced
2 tsp. salt
½ tsp. freshly ground pepper
¼ cup plus 2 Tbsp. packed brown sugar

Heat butter and oil in large cast iron skillet. Add sliced onions. Sauté until they begin to brown, about 10 minutes. Reduce heat and add salt and pepper. Cook partially covered, stirring frequently, until onions turn caramel color and are very soft, about 30 minutes. Add brown sugar and stir until dissolved. Serve warm.

Moderate

Serves 6–8
Preparation time:
10 minutes
Cook 40 minutes

A perfect accompaniment to any beef

Onion Pie

1½ cups Ritz® crackers, crushed
6 Tbsp. melted butter
2 cups onions, thinly sliced
2 eggs
¾ cup milk
¾ Tbsp. salt
Dash pepper
½ cup cheddar cheese, grated

Mix cracker crumbs and 4 Tbsp. butter. Press into 8 inch pie plate; chill. Sauté onions in 2 Tbsp. butter. Spoon into crust. Mix lightly beaten eggs with milk, salt and pepper and pour over onions. Sprinkle with cheese. Bake 30 minutes at 350°.

Easy

Serves 4–6
Preparation time:
20 minutes
Bake 30 minutes

An unusual accompaniment to steak

Potato Lasagna

2   large potatoes, peeled
    and halved crosswise
1   egg
1   cup ricotta cheese
1   8 oz. can tomato sauce
$\frac{1}{4}$ tsp. basil
$\frac{1}{4}$ tsp. oregano
Pinch of garlic powder
$\frac{1}{2}$ cup shredded mozzarella cheese

Cook potatoes in boiling water 10 minutes or until tender; drain and cool. Thinly slice potatoes. Combine egg and ricotta cheese. Combine tomato sauce, seasonings, and $\frac{1}{8}$ tsp. salt. Spray a 9x5x3 loaf dish with vegetable oil spray. Arrange half of the potato slices in bottom of pan. Spread half ricotta mixture, then half of the tomato sauce mixture over potatoes. Repeat layers. Sprinkle mozzarella cheese on top. Bake, covered, in a 400° oven 25 minutes or until potatoes are tender and lasagna is heated all the way through. Uncover, bake 5 minutes more.

Ratatouille

¹/₄ cup olive oil
4 cloves garlic
1 bay leaf
1 medium onion, chopped
2 medium bell peppers (any color), cubed
2 small zucchini (or 1 medium), cubed
1 small summer squash, cubed
3 Tbsp. dry red wine
¹/₂ cup tomato juice
1 tsp. basil
1 tsp. marjoram
¹/₂ tsp. oregano
Dash ground rosemary
2 tsp. salt
Pepper to taste
2 medium tomatoes, chopped
2 Tbsp. tomato paste
1 Tbsp. freshly chopped parsley

Easy

Serves 4–6
May prepare ahead
Preparation time:
 10 minutes
Cook 30 minutes

This is eggplant-less!

Serve as a side dish or as a vegetable stew with French bread.

Heat olive oil in a large, heavy skillet. Crush the garlic into the oil. Add bay leaf and onion; sauté over medium heat until onion becomes transparent. Add bell peppers, zucchini, and summer squash. Add wine, tomato juice, herbs, salt and pepper. Stir to mix well, cover and simmer 10 minutes. Add tomatoes and tomato paste; mix well. Continue to stew until vegetables are tender. Just before serving, mix in the fresh parsley.

Sautéed Cherry Tomatoes

1 Tbsp. unsalted butter
1 Tbsp. olive oil
2 cloves minced garlic
2 Tbsp. minced fresh basil or parsley
1 pint cherry tomatoes
Salt and pepper to taste

In a large skillet, melt butter on low heat; add olive oil and garlic and sauté until lightly browned. Add basil or parsley and tomatoes. Sauté until warmed thoroughly but not allowing the skins to tear. Add salt and pepper to taste.

Sautéed Red Bell Peppers

8 large sweet red bell peppers, cored, seeded and chopped
10 garlic cloves, chopped
2 Tbsp. chopped fresh oregano
$1/_3$ cup olive oil
Salt and pepper to taste
4 Tbsp. capers

Sauté red peppers in oil, oregano and garlic for 20 minutes or until cooked. Add salt and pepper to taste. Stir in capers.

Scalloped Potatoes Jurassien

2 lb. boiling potatoes, peeled and thinly sliced
1 tsp. salt
$^1/_2$ tsp. pepper
1 cup grated Emmental or domestic Swiss cheese
4 Tbsp. butter
$1^1/_2$ cups whipping cream

Moderate

Serves 8
Preparation time:
 30 minutes
Bake $1^1/_4$ hours

Grease flat flame proof casserole dish. Layer potatoes, sprinkle with salt, pepper, cheese and dots of butter. Pour cream over mixture and bring slowly to simmer on stove. Then place in middle of oven at 300° for $1^1/_4$ hours, never allowing cream to bubble. Potatoes are ready when tender, lightly browned on top and all cream is absorbed.

Serbian Spinach

Easy

Serves 12
May prepare ahead
Preparation time:
 5 minutes
Bake 1 hour

2   10 oz. pkg. frozen chopped spinach,
    cooked per directions
1   16 oz. carton small curd cottage cheese
1/4 cup butter, cut up
1/2 lb. cheddar cheese, grated
3   eggs, beaten
3   Tbsp. flour
1/4 tsp. salt

Mix all ingredients together, adding flour and salt last. Pour into well greased flat 2 quart baking dish. Bake at 350° about 1 hour until bubbly. May bake first 1/2 hour with lid or foil, then uncover for last 1/2 hour.   Do not brown top.

Spinach Supreme

Easy

Serves 4–6
Partially prepare
 ahead
Preparation time:
 30 minutes
Bake 30 minutes

2   10 oz. pkg. frozen chopped spinach,
    cooked and drained
1   5 oz. can water chestnuts,
    drained and thinly sliced
1   10 oz. pkg. frozen welsh rarebit, thawed
8   slices bacon, crisp cooked,
    drained and crumbled
1/2 3 1/2 oz. can french fried onion rings

This also makes a wonderful filling for baked tomatoes.

Combine spinach, water chestnuts, welsh rarebit and bacon. Spread in a 9x9 baking dish. (May be prepared to this point and refrigerated.) Bake uncovered at 350° for 20 minutes. Top with onion rings and bake for an additional 10 minutes.

Stir-fried Green Beans

1   lb. fresh green beans
4   Tbsp. peanut oil
2   cloves garlic, minced
1   cup chicken broth
1   tsp. salt

$\frac{1}{2}$ tsp. sugar
Dash of pepper
1   tsp. MSG (optional)
Dash of sesame seeds

Easy

Serves 4
Preparation time:
 10 minutes
Cook 15 minutes

Wash beans and cut diagonally into 1½ inch lengths. Place oil into wok, making sure it coats sides. Preheat wok with oil 2 minutes. Add green beans and garlic; stir-fry to coat beans with oil. Add chicken broth. Bring to boil. Reduce heat and cover wok. Cook 8 minutes, stirring occasionally. Add seasonings. Beans should be bright green, crisp, and crunchy.

Summer Corn

Easy

*Serves 6
Preparation time:
  15 minutes
Bake 30–45 minutes*

*Wonderful for a
buffet or with
grilled meat.*

6   ears fresh Silver Queen corn
1   green pepper, cut into 1" pieces
3   small green zucchini, sliced thickly
3   small yellow zucchini, sliced thickly
1   medium onion, chopped
4   fresh ripe tomatoes, unpeeled
    and thickly sliced
1   tsp. pepper medley
1   tsp. garlic salt
$\frac{1}{4}$ cup butter or margarine melted

With a very sharp knife cut corn from cob into
an oven proof casserole. Continue to make
layers with the remaining vegetables, ending
with the tomatoes. Season with garlic salt,
pepper medley and top with melted butter.
Cover and bake at 350° for 30 to 45 minutes.

Summer Squash
in the Microwave

2 Tbsp. butter
$\frac{1}{2}$ cup Towne House® or Ritz® cracker crumbs
$\frac{1}{4}$ cup water
$\frac{1}{2}$ tsp. salt
1 lb. yellow squash, sliced
1 egg, beaten
$\frac{1}{2}$–$\frac{3}{4}$ cup grated cheddar cheese
2 Tbsp. butter, melted
1 tsp. sugar
$\frac{1}{4}$ cup chopped onion

Easy

Serves 4
Preparation time:
 5 minutes
Cook 25 minutes

In 1-quart casserole, melt butter on high $\frac{1}{2}$–1 minute until melted; add crumbs and cook on high 2 minutes. Stir as needed. Set aside. Place water, salt and squash in casserole and cover. Cook on high 8–10 minutes or until tender. Stir as needed, drain squash. Mix remaining ingredients in casserole and add squash and cook uncovered at medium temperature for 4 minutes. Add crumb topping. Cook 2–4 minutes more until center is set. Let stand 5 minutes before serving.

Tailgate Beans

Moderate

Serves 6–8
May prepare ahead
Preparation time:
 15 minutes
Bake 1 hour

Great for tailgating
at football games

6–8 slices bacon
4   red hot smokey sausages, sliced
1   medium onion, chopped
1   16 oz. can baked beans, drained
1   16 oz. can butter beans, drained
1   16 oz. can kidney beans, drained
1   cup shredded cheddar cheese
$^1/_2$ cup brown sugar
$^3/_4$ cup ketchup
Dash of pepper
(Optional: 1 tsp. liquid BBQ smoke)

Cut bacon in small pieces. Slice sausages and fry together with bacon over medium heat. Add onion and cook until soft. Set aside. Drain liquid from beans. Combine all ingredients and stir well. Bake 1 hour at 350°.

Tomato Pudding

Easy

Serves 4
Preparation time:
 10 minutes
Bake 50 minutes

Serve as a side dish
with grilled salmon
or any fish

1   cup tomato purée
1   cup brown sugar
$^1/_4$ cup water
2   cups bread crumbs
$^1/_2$ cup butter, melted

Combine tomato purée, brown sugar and water; cook 5 minutes. While that mixture is cooking, place bread crumbs in a casserole dish. Pour butter over bread crumbs, then top with tomato mixture. Bake 50 minutes at 325° and serve immediately.

Vegetable Medley

2	pkg. frozen lima beans
2	cans blue lake green beans
2	pkg. frozen English peas
$1/4$	cup sliced almonds
$1/2$	cup grated cheddar cheese
$1/2$	pint whipping cream
$1/2$	cup mayonnaise or sour cream
Paprika	

Easy

Serves 8–10
May prepare ahead
Preparation time:
  15 minutes
Bake 20 minutes

Cook frozen lima beans as directed on package. In a flat casserole dish, combine cooked lima beans, green beans and peas. In a small bowl, combine whipping cream and mayonnaise. Pour over vegetables; stir. Top casserole with grated cheese and almonds. Sprinkle with paprika. Bake in 325° oven until cheese melts and almonds are toasted, about 20–30 minutes.

Vegetable Platter

Easy

Serves 6–8
May prepare ahead
Preparation time:
15 minutes

*Try this with green
beans, Belgian car-
rots, snow peas, ar-
tichoke hearts and
asparagus.*

$^1/_4$ cup wine vinegar
$^1/_4$ cup Crisco® oil
$^1/_2$ cup mayonnaise
$1^1/_2$ tsp. prepared mustard
$^1/_4$ tsp. salt
$^1/_4$ tsp. garlic powder
1 hard boiled eggs, sieved
4 Tbsp. chopped chives
Assorted fresh (steamed) or canned vegetables

Mix all ingredients, pour over your favorite assorted vegetables and refrigerate. Do not mix vegetables.

Baked Rice with Almonds

Easy

Serves 8–10
Preparation time:
5 minutes
Cook 55 minutes

*A great complement
to beef or chicken*

$^1/_2$ cup margarine
1 cup raw rice
1 pkg. slivered almonds
3 cups chicken broth (2 cans
or 3 cups water plus bouillon cubes)
2 Tbsp. chopped onion
1 small jar mushrooms
1 tsp. salt

Sauté almonds in 1 Tbsp. butter in large skillet. Combine other ingredients and stir in skillet for 3–5 minutes. Pour into casserole and cover. Bake at 350° for 50 minutes.

Fried Rice

3	Tbsp. bacon drippings
$\frac{1}{2}$	cup green onions and tops, diced
1	cup celery, diced
1	cup mushrooms, sliced
3	cups cooked rice (can be minute or long grain)
2	Tbsp. soy sauce
1	egg, slightly beaten
$\frac{1}{2}$	lb. crisp bacon, crumbled

Easy

Serves 4–6
Preparation time:
10 minutes
Cook 45 minutes

Heat bacon drippings in skillet. Add onions and celery, cook until tender. Add mushrooms, rice and soy sauce. Cook 10 minutes over low heat, stirring occasionally. Stir in beaten eggs and cook only until eggs are done. Add bacon and mix well. Cook 30 minutes on low heat. Extra soy sauce may be served with rice.

Oyster and Wild Rice Casserole

Moderate

Serves 8–10
Partially prepared
ahead
Preparation time:
 10 minutes
Cook 1 hour

Great for Thanks-
giving or Christmas

1	cup wild rice
2	cups water
2	cups chicken broth
1	small onion, chopped
3	ribs celery, chopped
$\frac{1}{2}$	cup unsalted butter
1	tsp. sage
1	tsp. thyme
$\frac{1}{4}$	tsp. each black, red and white pepper (to taste)
$\frac{1}{8}$	tsp. nutmeg
$\frac{1}{4}$	lb. mushrooms, sliced
1	bunch parsley, chopped
$1\frac{1}{2}$	pints oysters, drained
$\frac{1}{2}$	cup cracker crumbs
$\frac{1}{4}$	cup butter (melted)

Wash rice. Place rice, water, broth in large sauce pan and bring to a boil. Add onion, celery, butter, sage, thyme, peppers, nutmeg. Reduce heat, cover and simmer for 45 minutes. Fluff rice with fork and cook uncovered until all excess liquid evaporates. Add mushrooms and parsley. Put this mixture in 11x7 casserole dish. Melt butter and dip the oysters first in butter, then in cracker crumbs and arrange in rice. Bake uncovered for 15 minutes at 400°. Watch carefully to avoid overcooking oysters.

Wild Rice Casserole

1 cup uncooked wild rice, well rinsed
$^1/_2$ cup slivered almonds
2 Tbsp. chopped onion
8 oz. fresh mushrooms, sliced
$^1/_2$ cup butter
3 cups chicken broth

Easy

Serves 4
Preparation time:
10 minutes
Bake 1 hour

Heat oven to 325°. Combine all ingredients except chicken broth in heavy saucepan. Cook over medium heat, stir constantly until rice turns slightly yellow. Place into 1$^1/_2$ quart casserole, add broth. Bake covered at 325° for 1 hour.

Mayonnaise Sauce

1 can (water packed) tuna, drained
6 anchovies
$^1/_4$ cup lemon juice
$^3/_4$ cup olive oil

Easy

Yield: 1 cup
May prepare ahead
Preparation time:
10 minutes

Serve over tomatoes, cucumbers or cold chicken

Place tuna, anchovies and lemon juice in blender or food processor. Blend. Add olive oil a little at a time, blending until the consistency of mayonnaise.

Sauce for Red Beets

Easy

Yield: 6 cups
May prepare ahead
Preparation time:
 15 minutes
Cook 15 minutes

2 cups sugar
2 cups vinegar
2 cups water
1 Tbsp. cinnamon
1 tsp. cloves
1 tsp. allspice

Mix all ingredients together. Can either be simmered over already prepared red beets until heated through or poured over red beets, refrigerated and served cold.

Vegetable Sauce

Easy

Partially prepare
 ahead
Preparation time:
 15 minutes

Great on broccoli

$\frac{1}{2}$ cup mayonnaise
1 tsp. prepared mustard
$\frac{1}{4}$ tsp. instant minced onion
Hot vegetable of choice
$\frac{1}{2}$ cup shredded cheddar cheese

Mix mayonnaise, mustard and onion. Spoon over hot vegetable. Sprinkle with cheese. Cover and let stand until heated through and cheese is melted.

Eggs,
Cheese
and Pasta

Baked Eggs in Wild Rice

1	lb. sausage
$\frac{1}{4}$	cup butter
1	cup fresh mushrooms
1	bunch (6–8) green onions
$\frac{1}{8}$	tsp. each red, white, black pepper
$\frac{1}{2}$	tsp. dry mustard
4	cups cooked wild rice
2	cups cream
1	cup Velveeta® cheese
$\frac{1}{2}$	tsp. dry mustard
$\frac{1}{4}$	tsp. cayenne pepper
8	eggs

Moderate

Serves 8
*Partially prepare
 ahead*
*Preparation time:
 30 minutes*
*Bake 15 to 20
 minutes*

*A great brunch dish
especially in fall or
winter*

Cook sausage and drain. Melt butter in skillet; sauté mushrooms and green onions, add pepper. Combine cream and cheese in double boiler; cooking slowly. Add dry mustard and peppers to cheese mixture. Combine sausage, mushrooms and green onions with wild rice. Pour sausage mixture into 9x11 casserole dish; make eight indentations. Spoon cheese sauce into each indentation. Crack one egg into each indentation. Bake uncovered at 350° for 15 to 20 minutes, or until eggs are cooked as desired. Garnish with fresh parsley. Serve with baked fruit and muffins.

Blintz Soufflé

Easy

Serves 4 to 6
Preparation time:
 15 minutes
Bake 45 minutes

4 eggs, beaten
¼ lb. butter, melted
1½ cups sour cream
¼ cup sugar
1 tsp. vanilla
½ tsp. salt
1 Tbsp. orange juice
8 frozen blintzes (cheese, blueberry, apple, or cinnamon)
Powdered sugar

Spray vegetable oil spray onto the bottom of a 9x13 baking dish. In medium size bowl, beat together eggs, butter, sour cream, sugar, salt, vanilla, and orange juice. Space frozen blintzes evenly in baking dish. Pour egg mixture over blintzes. Bake at 350° for 45 minutes. Remove from oven and sprinkle with powdered sugar.

Brunch Casserole

Moderate

Serves 8
May prepare ahead
Preparation time:
 20 minutes
Bake 30 minutes

1 pkg. frozen shredded hash brown potatoes
12 eggs
2 Tbsp. dry parsley
1 lb. sausage, cooked and drained, or ½ lb. bacon, cooked and drained
1½ cups sour cream
2 small cans sliced mushrooms
1 bunch (6–8) green onions
2 Tbsp. butter
2 cups cheddar cheese, shredded

Cover hash browns with hot water and let stand 10 minutes. Drain hash browns well and pour into greased 9x13 pan. Scramble eggs with parsley to soft stage. Layer eggs over hash browns. Mix together sausage and sour cream. Layer sausage mixture over eggs. Sauté mushrooms and green onions in butter. Layer over sausage mixture. Top with cheddar cheese. Cover with foil and bake at 350° for 15 minutes. Uncover, bake 15 minutes more.

Eggs Benedict Arnold

¹/₄ cup butter
1   cup chopped seafood (shrimp, crab or lobster)
¹/₂ cup chopped fresh mushrooms
4   eggs
4   English muffins
Hollandaise sauce (bought or homemade)

Easy

Serves 2 to 4
Preparation time:
30 minutes
Cook 20 minutes

Melt butter in skillet and sauté seafood with mushrooms. Poach 4 eggs. Toast English muffins. Place muffins on plate and cover with seafood mixture. Top with poached egg. Pour Hollandaise sauce over top and serve.

Eggs Newport

Easy

Serves 4
Preparation time:
 20 minutes
Bake 20 minutes

1   10 oz. can cream of mushroom soup
$1/_2$ cup mayonnaise
$1/_2$ cup milk
1   tsp. chopped chives
6   hard boiled eggs
8   slices crisp bacon, crushed
4   toasted English muffins

Blend soup and mayonnaise. Gradually add milk and chives to soup mixture. Slice eggs and layer eggs and soup mixture in 1-quart baking dish. Sprinkle bacon over top. Bake 20 minutes at 350°. Serve over English muffins.

French Custard Toast

Easy

Serves 4
Partially prepare
 ahead
Preparation time:
 10 minutes
Soak overnight
Bake 16 minutes

Accompany with sugared bacon and fresh fruit

3   eggs
$1/_8$ tsp. nutmeg
1   cup whole milk
$1/_2$ tsp. salt
"Day old" French or Italian bread,
   sliced $1 1/_2$ inch thick

Beat eggs slightly with nutmeg in shallow pan or dish. Add milk and salt. Place bread in egg mixture and soak overnight. Bake at 500° for 8 minutes on each side. Serve with warm syrup or preserves.

Oeufs Enteralliés

1½ dozen eggs
½ lb. bacon
¼ cup butter
¼ cup flour
1 cup light cream
1 cup milk
1 lb. grated sharp cheddar cheese
1 small garlic clove, crushed
¼ tsp. thyme
¼ tsp. marjoram
¼ tsp. basil
¼ cup parsley
Buttered bread crumbs

Moderate

Serves 8
May prepare ahead
Preparation time:
 30 minutes
Bake 20-30 minutes

Hard cook eggs; peel and slice thinly. Sauté bacon until crisp; drain and crumble. Make cream sauce by combining butter, flour, light cream and milk. Heat sauce slowly, adding cheddar cheese. Stir until melted. Season sauce with garlic clove, thyme, marjoram and basil. Add parsley. Pour some of sauce into greased 8x11 baking dish. Add layers of egg slices, then bacon crumbles, and more cheese sauce. Continue until ingredients are used up, ending with sauce. Sprinkle with finely ground buttered bread crumbs. Bake at 350° for 20 to 30 minutes until bubbly and crumbs are browned. Garnish with fresh parsley.

Queen City Brunch

Easy

Serves 6-8
Prepare ahead
Preparation time:
 30 minutes
Refrigerate overnight
Bake 1 hour

Freezes well

12   slices white bread (crust removed)
Softened butter
³/₄   cup butter
2   cups yellow onions, sliced
³/₄   lb. fresh mushrooms, sliced
Salt
Pepper
1¹/₂   lb. mild Italian sausage
1   lb. cheddar cheese, grated
5   eggs
2¹/₂   cups milk
3¹/₂   tsp. Dijon mustard
1   tsp. dry mustard
1   tsp. nutmeg
2   Tbsp. fresh parsley

Butter bread slices and set aside. In skillet, sauté onions and mushrooms in butter until tender. Salt and pepper and set aside. Cook sausage and cut into bite-size pieces, drain. In greased 11x7 casserole, layer ¹/₂ the bread, ¹/₂ mushroom mixture, ¹/₂ sausage and ¹/₂ the cheese. Repeat layers, ending with cheese. Mix eggs, milk and seasonings together and pour over the layers. Cover and refrigerate overnight. When ready to bake, sprinkle with parsley over top and bake uncovered at 350° for 1 hour until bubbly.

Sausage, Zucchini, and Bell Pepper Frittata

¼ lb. spicy breakfast sausage
6 mushrooms, medium size, sliced
½ green pepper
1 zucchini, sliced
1 Tbsp. olive oil
1 tsp. dried basil, crumbled
¼ tsp. dried red pepper flakes
¼ tsp. salt
7 eggs, beaten
4 oz. mozzarella cheese, grated

Easy

Serves 4
Preparation time:
 30 minutes
Bake 25-30 minutes

Accompany with cornbread and salad for an easy summer meal.

Brown sausage in large skillet and drain. To skillet add mushrooms, green pepper, zucchini, oil, basil, pepper flakes, salt and sauté for 3 to 4 minutes. Add sausage mixture to eggs and cheese, combine. Pour mixture into 10 inch pie plate. Bake at 350° for 25–30 minutes or until eggs are set. Serve warm.

Spinach Pie

Easy

Serves 6
May prepare ahead
Preparation time:
 20 minutes
Bake 25 minutes

3 oz. pkg. cream cheese
1 cup half and half
1/2 cup soft bread cubes
1/4 cup grated Parmesan
2 eggs, beaten
1 cup cooked spinach, well-drained
 (or a 10 oz. frozen box)
4 Tbsp. butter
1 large onion chopped
1/2 lb. mushrooms, chopped
1 tsp. tarragon
3/4 tsp. salt
Unbaked 9 inch pastry shell

Mash cream cheese with a fork and gradually blend in half and half. Add bread cubes, Parmesan cheese, and eggs, beating with wire wisk to break up bread. Stir in spinach. Melt butter in skillet and sauté onions and mushrooms until lightly browned, stirring frequently. Add tarragon and blend onion mixture into cheese mixture. Salt to taste. Pour into pastry shell. Bake on lowest rack at 400° for 25 minutes until browned. Let stand 10 minutes before serving.

Swiss Cheese Scramble

8   slices bacon
2   cups soft bread cubes ($^1/_2$" cubes, no crusts)
1$^3/_4$ cups milk
8   eggs, slightly beaten
$^3/_4$ tsp. salt
$^1/_8$ tsp. pepper
4   Tbsp. butter
$^1/_4$ tsp. seasoned salt
$^1/_2$ lb. sliced Swiss cheese
$^1/_2$ cup dry bread crumbs

Easy

Serves 6
Preparation time:
 30 minutes
Bake 15 minutes

A no-fail brunch
delight

Fry bacon until crisp and crumble. Combine bread cubes with milk. Drain after 5 minutes and set aside. Combine milk with eggs, salt and pepper. Melt 2 Tbsp. butter in skillet, and scramble egg mixture until soft (not fully cooked). Add soaked bread cubes and turn into 9" baking dish. Sprinkle with seasoned salt. Arrange Swiss cheese over top. Combine 2 Tbsp. butter (melted) and dry bread crumbs and sprinkle over top. Top with crumbled bacon. Bake at 400° for 10–15 minutes.

Tomato Quiche

Easy

Serves 6 to 8
May prepare ahead
Preparation time:
 20 minutes
Bake 45 minutes

Freezes well

1	large can tomatoes, drained and chopped
1	medium onion, chopped
3	Tbsp. butter
1	tsp. salt
1/4	tsp. thyme
1/2	lb. Swiss cheese, diced
3	eggs
1	cup half and half

Lightly grease an 8x10 baking dish. Cook tomatoes, onion, butter, salt, and thyme until reduced by half—about 10 minutes. Place Swiss cheese in baking dish. Pour tomato mixture evenly over cheese. Combine eggs with half and half, beat well and pour over tomato mixture. Bake at 425° for 10 minutes, then reduce temperature to 375° for 35 minutes.

Gnocchi à la Romaine

1   quart milk
½   cup butter
1   cup hominy grits (not quick)
⅛   tsp. pepper
⅓   cup butter, melted
1   cup grated Gruyère cheese
⅓   cup freshly grated Parmesan cheese

Bring milk to a boil. Add ½ cup butter, cut into pieces. Gradually stir in the grits and resume boiling until mixture looks like cooked farina. Remove from heat, add salt and pepper and beat hard with electric mixer until grits take on a creamy appearance. Pour into 13x9x2 pan. Allow to set. Cut into rectangular pieces. Place them one over another like rows of fallen dominoes in buttered shallow casserole that can be brought to the table. Pour melted butter over grits and sprinkle with the grated cheeses. At serving time (which can be next day), bake uncovered in 400° oven for 30 minutes until bubbly and light brown.

Moderate

Serves 8
May prepare ahead
Preparation time:
 20 minutes
Bake 30 minutes

Freezes well

Good as a brunch side dish or with ham or beef

Cappelini, Tomatoes, and Fresh Basil Sauce

Easy

Serves 6 to 8
Partially prepare
  ahead
Preparation time:
  5 minutes
Cook 20 minutes

Great summer dish
along with grilled
chicken, zucchini
squash and green
salad.

2   lb. fresh tomatoes, peeled or canned
      plum tomatoes
1   cup fresh basil, coarsely chopped
3   Tbsp. sherry vinegar or 2 Tbsp.
      white vinegar plus 1 Tbsp. sherry
1³/₄ oz. jar of capers, drained and rinsed
Salt and pepper
1   lb. cappelini pasta
³/₄ cup olive oil

To coarsely chopped tomatoes add basil; let stand 1 to 2 hours at room temperature or overnight in refrigerator. Before serving, blend vinegar, capers, salt and pepper into tomato mixture which should be at room temperature. Cook pasta al dente, drain, and transfer to serving platter. Add olive oil to pasta and toss gently. Mix in tomato sauce with pasta. Let stand 5 minutes before serving.

Fettuccine Alfredo

1   cup unsalted butter
$^1/_4$ cup heavy cream
$^3/_4$ cup parmesan cheese
$^1/_2$ lb. fettuccine
Black pepper to taste

Easy

Serves 6
Partially prepare
  ahead
Preparation time:
  10 minutes
Cook 10 minutes

Soften butter. Beat until smooth. Add cream gradually and beat well. Add $^1/_2$ cup Parmesan cheese and beat well. Boil noodles until tender. Drain noodles well and add Alfredo sauce, mix well. Sprinkle with lots of black pepper and $^1/_4$ cup Parmesan cheese.

Note: Alfredo sauce may be made ahead of time and refrigerated. Sauce must be removed from refrigerator at least 1 hour prior to mixing with fettuccine.

Fettuccine with Three Cheeses and Pistachios

Moderate

Serves 8
Preparation time:
 30 minutes
Cook 20 minutes

Extremely rich! May substitute any type of pasta

2   Tbsp. shelled natural pistachios
$^3/_4$ cup unsalted butter, softened
$^1/_2$ lb. sweet Gorgonzola cheese, crumbled
Dash salt
$^1/_2$ lb. mozzarella cheese, diced
$^1/_2$ lb. fontina cheese
2   lb. fresh fettuccine (or 1 lb. dry)
Freshly ground pepper

Blanch pistachios in boiling water 15 seconds; immediately rinse under cold water; drain. Slip off skins; spread on paper towels to dry. Combine butter and Gorgonzola in medium bowl; beat until blended and almost whipped in consistency. Heat large kettle of water to boiling; add salt. Combine mozzarella and fontina cheeses in a large, heavy saucepan. Cook, stirring frequently, over low heat until cheeses are melted. Stir in pistachios; remove from heat. Cook pasta in boiling water until al dente (fresh pasta only requires 15–30 seconds). Drain pasta thoroughly, add to cheese in saucepan. Place over medium heat; stir until pasta is completely coated with cheese mixture. Add pepper to taste. Remove from heat, stir in butter/Gorgonzola mixture until melted. Serve immediately.

Linguine au Legumes

2	cups fresh broccoli florets
1	cup fresh asparagus, cut into 1 inch pieces
1	cup sliced mushrooms
$\frac{1}{2}$	cup Chinese snow peas
$\frac{1}{2}$	cup frozen green peas, thawed
1	garlic clove, diced
6	Tbsp. butter
12	oz. linguine pasta
$\frac{3}{4}$	cup half and half
1	cup Parmesan cheese
4	Tbsp. butter, softened
$\frac{1}{4}$	tsp. salt
$\frac{1}{4}$	tsp. pepper

Easy

Serves 8 to 10
Preparation time:
* 20 minutes*
Cook 20 minutes

Great with grilled
fish or chicken.

Cook pasta. While pasta is cooking, sauté the broccoli, asparagus, mushrooms, pea pods, green peas and garlic clove in the 6 Tbsp. of butter. Drain pasta and toss with sautéed vegetables. Add remaining ingredients and toss again. Serve immediately.

Marinara Sauce

Moderate

Serves 6
May prepare ahead
Preparation time:
 30 minutes
Cook 2¹/₂ hours

Freezes well

This makes a wonderful first course to a meal.

4   large cans Italian plum tomatoes with basil
4¹/₂ Tbsp. Crisco® oil
2   whole cloves garlic, peeled
1   Tbsp. dried basil
Pinch of sugar
Salt and pepper to taste
1¹/₂ lb. angel hair pasta
Parmesan cheese

Put tomatoes through a food mill or mash through a strainer to remove all seeds. Heat oil and whole garlic cloves. Sauté until brown. Add tomatoes to oil and garlic. Add basil (crush between hands). Add salt, pepper and small pinch of sugar. Cook for 1 hour, partially covered over low heat. Simmer for 1¹/₂ hours uncovered, stirring occasionally. Serve over angel hair pasta topped with Parmesan cheese.

Pasta Pronto

7	oz. pkg. elbow macaroni or other small pasta
4	cups chicken, cooked and cut into bite size pieces
$\frac{1}{2}$	cup celery, diced
$\frac{1}{2}$	lb. cheddar cheese, grated
2	cans cream of chicken soup
1	pint half and half
$\frac{1}{4}$	cup green pepper, chopped
3	Tbsp. sherry or $\frac{1}{2}$ tsp. curry powder (optional)

Combine all ingredients. Pour into buttered 3 quart casserole or baking dish. Cover and let stand overnight in refrigerator. Bake at 350° for 1 hour or until bubbly.

Easy

Serves 8
Prepare ahead
Preparation time:
 25 minutes
Chill overnight
Bake 1 hour

Freezes well

Substitute shrimp and cream of shrimp soup for a delightful change.

Pasta Puttanesca

Moderate

Serves 4
Preparation time:
 15 minutes
Cook 15 minutes

Serve with an earthy
red wine.

9	oz. Angel hair pasta
1	eggplant, peeled and diced
1/2	cup olive oil
1/3	2.8 oz. tube sun dried tomato paste
5	gloves garlic, crushed
1	tsp. oregano
1	tsp. basil
1/4	tsp. red pepper (or to taste)
1	cup parsley
1/2	cup black olives
8	anchovy fillets, chopped
1/4	cup drained capers

Bring water to boil and add pasta. Cook until tender but firm. Transfer to heated plates. Combine eggplant, olive oil, sun dried tomato paste, garlic, oregano, basil, red pepper and parsley. Cook until eggplant is done. Fold in black olives, anchovies and capers. Serve over hot pasta.

Pesto Sauce

2   cups tightly packed fresh basil leaves
      (in winter, substitute 1½ cups parsley
      and 2 Tbsp. dried basil)
¼   cup freshly grated Parmesan cheese
4   garlic cloves, halved
1   Tbsp. pine nuts
Salt and pepper to taste
⅔   cup olive oil

Combine all ingredients except oil in food processor or blender. Blend, adding olive oil slowly until sauce is thick and smooth.

Easy

Yield: 2 cups
May prepare ahead
Preparation time:
* 10 minutes*

Freezes well

May be served with any kind of pasta.

Spaghetti and Meatballs

Moderate

Serves 6 to 8
May prepare ahead
Preparation time:
45 minutes
Cook 2 hours

Freezes well

Meatballs:
1½ lb. ground beef
1   egg, beaten
¼   cup water
1½ tsp. salt
½   tsp. basil leaves, crushed
¼   tsp. pepper
½   cup fine dry bread crumbs
¼   cup Parmesan cheese

Sauce:
2   1 lb. cans whole tomatoes
2   6 oz. cans tomato paste
1   cup water
¼   cup onion, chopped
1   garlic clove, minced
2   Tbsp. parsley
2   tsp. oregano
1   tsp. salt
¼   tsp. anise seed or ⅛ tsp. fennel seed

Meatballs:
Break meat up with a fork and combine with egg, water, salt, basil and pepper. To meat mixture add bread crumbs and cheese. Shape into 1 inch balls. Brown in an ungreased skillet.

Sauce:
Combine tomatoes, tomato paste, water, onion, garlic, parsley, oregano, salt, and anise or fennel seed in a deep pan. Add meatballs and drippings. Bring to a boil; cover, simmer gently 2 hours until thick and glossy, stirring occasionally. Serve over pasta.

Spaghetti Carbonara

8 oz. thin spaghetti
$^1/_2$ lb. bacon, cut into 1 inch pieces
$^2/_3$ cup chopped green onions
4 oz. sliced mushrooms, drained
$^1/_4$ cup butter
$^1/_2$ cup Parmesan cheese, freshly shredded
$^1/_2$ cup sharp cheddar cheese, shredded
$^1/_8$ tsp. salt
Dash of pepper
3 egg yolks, lightly beaten

Easy

Serves 4 to 6
Preparation time:
 15 minutes
Cook 20 minutes

In a large pot, cook pasta, drain, and keep warm. In a large skillet, cook bacon until crisp. Remove bacon from skillet, reserving 2 Tbsp. of drippings, and add green onions and mushrooms. Sauté onions and mushrooms over low heat for 2 minutes; set aside with bacon. In same skillet, melt butter and add spaghetti, bacon, onions, mushrooms, cheeses and seasonings; toss lightly with a fork to combine. Add egg yolks gradually and mix well. Remove from heat and serve immediately.

Spaghetti sans Tomato Sauce

Easy

Serves 2
Preparation time:
  30 minutes

230 calories
per serving

3   cups cooked spaghetti
6   oz. Canadian bacon
2   eggs
3   Tbsp. milk
4   Tbsp. Romano cheese, grated
2   Tbsp. parsley, freshly minced
$1^1/_4$ tsp. oregano or Italian seasonings
Salt and pepper to taste

Cook spaghetti in boiling water until tender. While pasta is cooking, dice Canadian bacon and brown in a non-stick pan. Drain spaghetti. Beat eggs in milk and stir into spaghetti. Add bacon, cheese and seasonings. Serve immediately.

Stuffed Pasta Shells

1   12 oz. box jumbo pasta shells
2   9 or 10 oz. pkg. frozen creamed spinach in boiling bag
16 oz. ricotta cheese
8   oz. mozzarella cheese, grated
1   32 oz. jar of spaghetti sauce or sauce of your choice

Easy

Serves 8
May prepare ahead
Preparation time:
 25 minutes
Bake 1 hour
 20 minutes

Freezes well

Do not pre-cook shells. Prepare spinach as per package directions. Combine spinach, ricotta cheese, and mozzarella cheese. Pour some spaghetti sauce in bottom of 9x13 baking dish. Stuff shells with spinach mixture and place in baking dish. Cover with remaining sauce. Cover with foil and bake at 350° for 1 hour 20 minutes or until shells are tender.

Vegetarian Lasagne

Moderate

Serves 8-10
May prepare ahead
Preparation time:
 45 minutes
Bake 30 minutes

8　oz. lasagne noodles
2　lb. fresh spinach
3　cups mushrooms, freshly sliced
1　cup grated carrots
$^1/_2$　cup chopped onion
1　Tbsp. Crisco® oil
1　15 oz. can tomato sauce
1　6 oz. can tomato paste
1　15 oz. can pitted black olives, sliced
$1^1/_2$ tsp. oregano
2　cups cottage cheese
16　oz. Monterey Jack cheese, shredded

Cook lasagne noodles 8-10 minutes; drain. Rinse spinach and cook covered on medium heat until steam forms; reduce heat and simmer 3-5 minutes uncovered. In a large skillet, sauté mushrooms, carrots and onions in oil until tender. Stir tomato sauce, tomato paste, olives, and oregano into mushroom mixture. Reserve some Monterey Jack cheese for topping. In a 9x13 baking dish, layer $^1/_2$ noodles, $^1/_2$ cottage cheese, $^1/_2$ spinach, $^1/_2$ Monterey Jack cheese, and $^1/_2$ tomato mushroom mixture. Repeat layers and top with reserved Monterey Jack. Bake at 375° for 30 minutes. Let stand 10 minutes before serving.

Zesta Spaghetti

2   Tbsp. butter
7   oz. can white tuna in oil or 1 can water-
    packed tuna plus 3 Tbsp. olive oil.
    Generous amounts of milled black pepper
2   oz. can anchovies, drained and chopped
3   tsp. capers
1   lb. spaghetti

In saucepan, melt butter. Stir in tuna with oil and break into small pieces. Add milled pepper, anchovies, capers, and simmer 15 minutes, stirring occasionally. Cook spaghetti al dente, omitting the salt from cooking water. Drain spaghetti and toss into saucepan with tuna mixture, coating pasta well. Serve immediately.

Easy

Serves 4-6
Preparation time:
 10 minutes
Cook 20 minutes

Breads

Anadama Bread

3½-4 cups flour
1 pkg. active dry yeast
⅓ cup yellow cornmeal
1½ cups boiling water
⅓ cup molasses, light or dark
¼ cup shortening or sweet butter
1 Tbsp. salt
1 egg

Moderate

Yield: 1 loaf
Preparation time:
 4 hours 45 minutes
Bake 30 minutes

Freezes well

In a large bowl, mix 2 cups flour and yeast. Gradually stir cornmeal into boiling water. Add molasses, shortening and salt. Cool to lukewarm. Combine cornmeal and flour mixture. Add egg. Beat at low speed with the electric mixer for 1 minute. Beat at high speed for 2 minutes. By hand, stir in enough remaining flour to make a soft dough. Knead on a floured board until smooth and elastic (about 5 minutes). Place in lightly buttered bowl. Turn once to butter surface. Cover and let rise until double in bulk. Punch dough down. Cover and let rest 10 minutes. Pat dough down to flatten. Roll into loaf shape to fit bread pan. Grease 9½x5¼ pan. Put dough in pan. Cover and let rise until double. Bake at 400° for 25–30 minutes. Remove immediately from pan. Cool on wire rack.

Apricot Nut Bread

Moderate

Yield: 1 large or 2 small loaf pans
Preparation time:
 1 hour
Bake 1 hour

Freezes well

1   cup dried apricots
1   cup sugar
2   Tbsp. melted Crisco® or Crisco® oil
1   egg
$\frac{1}{4}$ cup water
$\frac{1}{4}$ cup orange juice
2   cups flour
2   tsp. baking powder
1   tsp. salt
$\frac{1}{2}$ tsp. baking soda
$\frac{1}{2}$ cup chopped pecans

Preheat oven to 350°. Soak apricots approximately 30 minutes in water. Drain and cut into $\frac{1}{4}$" pieces. Cream shortening and sugar; add egg. Stir in water and juice. Stir in sifted dry ingredients. Add nuts and apricots. Let stand 20 minutes. Grease one large loaf pan or two small loaf pans. Pour mixture into pan(s). Bake 45–60 minutes at 350°.

Brew Bread

Easy

Yield: 1 loaf
Preparation time:
 10 minutes
Bake 45 minutes

3   cups self-rising flour
3   Tbsp. sugar
1   can beer, never chilled
1   Tbsp. Crisco® oil

Preheat oven to 375°. Mix, with a spoon, flour, sugar and beer. Place in a greased bread pan. Spread 1 Tbsp. salad oil on top of dough for ease of slicing. Bake at 375° for 30 minutes, then reduce temperature to 325° for 15 minutes. Serve warm.

Great with a steak dinner!

Cheese and Onion Cornbread

4   medium onions, sliced
6   Tbsp. butter
2   8$\frac{1}{2}$ oz. boxes corn muffin mix
1   can cream style corn
1   cup sour cream
1   cup grated sharp cheddar cheese

Preheat oven to 350°. Sauté onions in butter. Pour butter into a 9x13 baking dish. Add corn muffin mix prepared as box directs but substitute creamed corn for milk. Turn into buttered dish. Top with layered onions, sour cream and cheddar. Bake 40 minutes at 350°.

Moderate

Serves 8
Preparation time:
* 15–20 minutes*
Bake 40 minutes

Freezes well

Great with a
"country" meal

Cheese Bread

Easy

Yield: 1 loaf
Preparation time:
 2 hours
Bake 15–20 minutes

Freezes well

1   lb. frozen loaf of bread dough,
     or your own
8–12 oz. grated sharp cheddar cheese
$^1/_2$ cup milk
1   egg, beaten
Pinch of dry mustard

Thaw dough according to package directions. Grease an $8^1/_2$x11 or 9x13 dish. Pat dough into pan. Mix cheese, milk, egg and mustard. Spread cheese mixture over the bread dough. Cover dish with plastic wrap and let rise until doubled in bulk (approximately $1^1/_2$–2 hours). Remove plastic wrap and bake bread in a 350° oven for 15–20 minutes. Let bread rest about 15 minutes before serving.

Cinnamon-Carrot Bread

$^3/_4$ cup sugar
$^1/_4$ cup brown sugar
$^3/_4$ cup Crisco® oil
2 cups all purpose flour
2 tsp. baking powder
1 tsp. baking soda
1 tsp. cinnamon
2 eggs, beaten
1 cup grated carrots
$^3/_4$ cups chopped pecans
$^1/_2$ tsp. vanilla extract

Preheat oven to 350°. In a large bowl, beat together the sugars and the oil. Sift together the flour, baking powder, baking soda and cinnamon into a bowl. Mix well. Gradually add 2 beaten eggs. Stir in grated carrots, chopped pecans and vanilla extract; combine well. Pour batter into a greased 9x5 loaf pan. Bake on the middle rack of a 350° oven for 1 hour. Remove from oven and let stand for 10 minutes before turning onto a rack to cool.

Easy

Yield: 9x5 loaf
Preparation time:
* 30 minutes*
Bake 1 hour

Freezes well

A good snack for
after school

Cowboy Bread

Easy

Serves 12–16
Preparation time:
  15 minutes
Bake 30 minutes

Freezes well

$1^1/_4$ cups sifted flour
1 cup brown sugar (light or dark)
$^1/_4$ tsp. salt
$^3/_8$ cup butter
1 tsp. baking powder
$^1/_4$ tsp. cinnamon
$^1/_4$ tsp. nutmeg
$^1/_2$ tsp. baking soda
$^1/_2$ cup sour milk (milk may be soured by taking $1^1/_2$ tsp. milk out of the $^1/_2$ cup and replacing it with $1^1/_2$ tsp. vinegar; wait 10 minutes.)
2 well beaten eggs

Combine first 4 ingredients in a large bowl. Rub between hands to make fine crumbs. Save $^1/_2$ cup of the mixture to sprinkle on top. Add next 3 ingredients to remaining crumbs. Dissolve the soda in the sour milk in a separate bowl. Add the eggs. Stir soda, milk and egg mixture into the crumbs; mix until smooth. Pour into a greased 8x8 pan. Sprinkle with crumbs. Bake at 375° for about 30 minutes. Cut into squares and serve.

Dinner Rolls
from the Freezer

5–6 cups flour
$^1/_2$ cup sugar
Dash of salt
2 pkg. dry yeast
$1^1/_4$ cups water
$^1/_4$ cup milk
5 Tbsp. butter
2 eggs

Moderate

*Yield: approx.
4 dozen
Preparation time:
3 hours
Bake 15 minutes*

Freezes well

In mixer or food processor, mix 2 cups flour, sugar, salt and undissolved yeast. Combine water, milk and butter and heat to 125° (a microwave temperature probe will help). Add liquids to flour mixture. Mix or process. Add eggs and enough flour to make a soft, non-sticky dough. Let dough rest, covered, for about 20 minutes. Punch down. Roll dough out $^1/_2$" thick and cut with a round cookie cutter. Fold circles in half and place on greased baking sheet. Cover with plastic wrap and freeze. Store in freezer until ready to use.

To bake: Cover and let rise in a warm place until doubled in bulk, about 2 hours. Bake at 350° for 15 minutes.

Heavenly Butterscotch Rolls

Moderate

Yield: 12–18 rolls
Preparation time:
 3 hours
Bake 20 minutes

Freezes well

1 cup milk, heated to scalding
2 Tbsp. butter
2 Tbsp. sugar
Pinch of salt
1 cake of yeast
1 egg, separated
3 cups sifted flour, divided
1 stick butter, melted
1¹/₂–2 cups brown sugar

Mix milk, butter, sugar and salt together in a mixing bowl and cool to lukewarm. Beat in yeast, egg yolk and 1¹/₂ cups flour, mixing until smooth. Beat egg white until stiff, then add to bowl alternately with 1¹/₂ cups more flour. Let dough rise in a warm place 1¹/₂–2 hours. Roll dough to ¹/₂" thickness. Spread with melted butter and half of the brown sugar. Roll up into a long roll and pull into an even shape. Cut 1" pieces and place flat in pan that has melted butter and balance of the brown sugar in the bottom. Let rolls rise ¹/₂ hour. Bake in 400° oven for 20 minutes.

Holiday Cranberry Bread

2 cups flour
¹/₂ tsp. salt
1¹/₂ tsp. baking powder
1 cup sugar
¹/₂ tsp. baking soda
1 egg, beaten
2 Tbsp. butter, melted
¹/₂ cup orange juice
¹/₂ cup nuts, finely chopped
1¹/₂ cups fresh cranberries
1 Tbsp. lemon rind, grated

Preheat oven to 350°. Sift together dry ingredients. Stir in remaining ingredients. Pour into a greased loaf pan and bake at 350° for 1 hour. Wrap in aluminum foil while lukewarm.

Easy

Yield: 1 loaf
Preparation time:
* 30 minutes*
Bake 1 hour

A delicious holiday gift or picnic bread.

Because berries are left whole, it makes a pretty picture when served.

To take to a picnic, slice, butter and rewrap in foil.

Parmesan Casserole Bread

Moderate

Serves 6–8
Preparation time:
 1 hour
Bake 20–25 minutes

1   pkg. active dry yeast
$\frac{1}{4}$ cup warm water
$\frac{1}{4}$ cup scalded milk
$1\frac{1}{2}$ cups sifted flour
1   Tbsp. sugar
$\frac{1}{2}$ tsp. salt
$\frac{1}{3}$ cup butter
1   egg, beaten
$\frac{1}{2}$ cup Parmesan cheese, grated
1   Tbsp. chopped parsley

Soften yeast in warm water. Cool milk to luke-warm. Meanwhile, sift flour, sugar and salt into large mixing bowl. With pastry blender, cut in butter until mixture resembles coarse meal. Add egg, yeast, and milk; beat well. Stir in the cheese and parsley. Turn into greased 8x1$\frac{1}{2}$ round pan. Cover with damp cloth and let rise until double, about 40 minutes. Dot with additional butter. Bake at 375° for 20–25 minutes. Cut into pie shaped wedges. Serve warm.

Peach Bread

1½ cups sugar

½ cup Crisco®

2 eggs

2¼ cups fresh peach puree (6–8 medium peaches with skins on, put through blender, or 3 15 oz. cans of peaches, drained.

2 cups flour

1 tsp. cinnamon

1 tsp. baking soda

1 tsp. baking powder

¼ tsp. salt

1 tsp. almond extract

1 cup chopped pecans

Preheat oven to 325°. Cream sugar and shortening. Add eggs and mix well. Add peach puree, dry ingredients, and almond flavoring. Add nuts and mix thoroughly. Pour into two 9x5 greased loaf pans. Bake at 325° 50–60 minutes.

Easy

Yield: 2 9x5 loaves
Preparation time:
15 minutes
Bake 50–60 minutes

Freezes well

The perfect use for over-ripe peaches.

Peach butter is a delicious accompaniment and can be made by simply mixing peach jam and softened butter.

Spoon Bread

Moderate

Serves 6
Preparation time:
  20 minutes
Bake 35 minutes

1   cup cornbread mix
$^1/_2$ tsp. salt
2   cups milk
3   beaten egg yolks
3   stiffly beaten whites

Combine cornbread mix and salt in a 2 quart saucepan. Gradually stir in milk until smooth. Cook over medium heat, stirring constantly until very thick—about 3–5 minutes. Blend $^1/_2$ cup cooked mixture into egg yolks. Blend in remaining cooked mixture until smooth. Fold in egg whites. Bake in greased round $1^1/_2$ quart casserole at 350° for 30–35 minutes or until knife inserted in center comes out clean. Serve immediately.

Strawberry Nut Bread with Strawberry Butter

Easy

Yield: 2 9x5 loaves
  or 5 mini loaves
Preparation time:
  15–20 minutes
Bake 50–60 minutes

Freezes well

3   cups all purpose flour
2   cups sugar
1   tsp. baking soda
1   tsp. salt
1   tsp. cinnamon
1   cup chopped nuts of choice
4   eggs, beaten
$^1/_4$ cup Crisco® oil
2   10 oz. pkg. frozen strawberries, drained
    (reserve juice)

Butter:

$^1/_2$ cup butter

$^1/_2$ cup strawberry juice

$^3/_4$ cup powdered sugar

Preheat oven to 350°. Grease and flour choice of 2 large or 5 mini loaf pans. Combine all dry ingredients in a large bowl; make a well in the center. Stir in beaten eggs, oil, and strawberries; mix well. Pour into loaf pans and bake 50–60 minutes for large loaves; 20–25 minutes for mini loaves. Cool 10 minutes in pan, remove, cool on rack.

Butter:

Combine all ingredients and mix well, or use food processor.

Sweet and Sour Lemon Bread

Easy

Yield: 9x5 loaf
Preparation time:
 25 minutes
Bake 1 hour

6 Tbsp. butter
1 cup sugar
2 beaten eggs
1½ cups sifted flour
1 tsp. baking powder
Dash of salt
½ cup milk
Grated rind of one lemon
¼ cup sugar
Juice of one lemon

Preheat oven to 375°. Cream butter and 1 cup of sugar; add eggs. Sift together flour, baking powder and salt. Add dry ingredients to egg mixture alternately with milk, in a few swift strokes. Add rind and beat until blended. Bake in a greased loaf pan for 1 hour at 375°. Meanwhile, mix ¼ cup sugar with lemon juice. When loaf is hot from the oven, prick a few times with a toothpick and pour juice mixture over the bread.

Swiss-French Bread

Moderate

Yield: 1 loaf
Preparation time:
 2 hours 20 minutes
Bake 30 minutes

1 pkg. dry yeast
1 tsp. sugar
1 cup warm water
2 cups flour
½ cup cake flour
1 tsp. salt
½ cup shredded Swiss cheese

1   Tbsp. Crisco® oil and some corn meal
1   egg
1   Tbsp. cream

Mix yeast, sugar and water together to proof. It will begin to bubble after 10 minutes. Combine the flours and salt. Place 2 cups of flour mixture in the food processing bowl. Add about half of the liquid and turn on/off 5 times. Add remainder of the liquid, most of the flour and the cheese; turn on/off 5 times; then allow the machine to run until the dough forms a non-sticky ball. If it is sticky, add a little flour until dough is only slightly sticky. Place the ball of dough into a well-oiled ceramic bowl. Turn the dough over and cover the bowl with a damp cloth. Place in a warm place (75–80°) until doubled in bulk, about 1 hour.

Remove to a lightly floured board and roll out into a rectangle; punch bubbles. Form loaf by rolling the dough tightly and make the seam tight. Press ends under the loaf. Place loaf with the seam side down on a French bread pan which has been brushed with oil and cornmeal. Slash the loaf diagonally on the top. Cover with a damp cloth and allow to rise 1 hour, again. Brush loaf with glaze made by combining the cream and egg. Bake at 400° for 30 minutes until loaf is brown.

Cinnamon-Pecan Coffee Cake

Easy

Serves 12-24
Preparation time:
 25 minutes
Bake 35–40 minutes

Cake:
$1/_2$	cup butter, softened
1	cup sugar
2	eggs
$1^1/_2$	tsp. vanilla
2	cups sifted flour
1	tsp. baking soda
1	tsp. baking powder
$1/_2$	tsp. salt
1	cup sour cream

Topping:
$1/_3$	cup brown sugar
$1/_2$	cup granulated sugar
1	tsp. cinnamon
1	cup chopped pecans

Preheat oven to 325°. Grease 9x13 pan. Combine first 4 ingredients; set aside. Sift flour, soda, baking powder and salt; add to butter mixture. Add sour cream. Spread $1/_2$ the batter in pan. Combine topping ingredients; sprinkle $1/_2$ the topping over the batter. Repeat layers with batter and topping. Bake at 325° for 35 minutes, or until toothpick comes out clean.

St. Pete's Coffee Cake

1   pkg. yellow cake mix
1   3 oz. pkg. instant vanilla or
    French vanilla pudding mix
1/2 cup Crisco® oil
1   cup sour cream or milk
4   eggs

Sugar Mixture:
1/4 cup granulated sugar
1/4 cup light brown sugar
1/2 cup ground or broken nuts
1   Tbsp. cinnamon

Easy

Serves 20
Preparation time:
 20 minutes
Bake 1 hour and
 10 minutes

Freezes well

Preheat oven to 325°. Combine cake mix, pudding, oil, sour cream and eggs. Beat at low speed until blended, then medium speed for several minutes. Fold sugar mixture into batter. (Reserve 3 Tbsp. of sugar mixture for topping.) Pour into lightly greased tube pan and sprinkle remaining 3 Tbsp. of sugar mixture on top. Bake in preheated oven at 325° for one hour; 5–10 minutes longer if needed. Cool before removing from the pan.

Susie's Coffee Cake

Easy

Serves 12–16
Preparation time:
 15 minutes
Bake 45 minutes

Freezes well

A non-yeast
quick bread

$^1/_2$ cup Crisco®
1   cup sugar
2   eggs
1   tsp. vanilla
1   tsp. baking soda
1   cup sour cream
$1^1/_2$ cups flour
$1^1/_2$ tsp. baking powder
$^1/_2$ tsp. salt
1   tsp. cinnamon
$^1/_3$ cup sugar
$^1/_4$ cup chopped nuts

Preheat oven to 350°. Cream shortening, sugar, eggs and vanilla. Stir together baking soda and sour cream, add to first mixture. Stir together flour, baking powder and salt. Add dry ingredients to the batter. Put $^1/_2$ batter into greased tube pan. Mix cinnamon, sugar and nuts for topping. Sprinkle $^1/_2$ topping over the batter in the pan. Add remaining batter. Top with remaining cinnamon mixture. Swirl lightly and bake at 350° for 45 minutes. Turn off oven and allow the cake to cool with oven door open.

Chocolate Waffles

2 cups flour
$^1/_2$ cup cocoa
$^1/_4$ cup sugar
3 tsp. baking powder
$^1/_2$ tsp. salt
3 eggs, separated
$1^1/_4$ cups milk
$^1/_4$ cup melted butter

Sift dry ingredients together. Beat egg yolks and add to dry ingredients, along with milk and melted butter. Stir until smooth. Beat egg whites until stiff and fold in gently. Cook on greased waffle iron.

Easy

Serves 6–8
Preparation time:
15 minutes
Cook 10 minutes

Serve with powdered sugar and fresh fruit.

Grandma's Waffles

Easy

Serves 4–5
Preparation time:
  10–15 minutes
Cook 3–5 minutes

Freezes well

2 cups flour
$^1/_2$ tsp. salt
3 tsp. baking powder
2 eggs
$1^3/_4$ cups milk
4–6 Tbsp. melted Crisco®, cooled

Sift all dry ingredients into a large bowl. Separate eggs. Add yolks to the milk, mix. Beat milk mixture into dry ingredients. Add Crisco®. Beat egg whites until stiff; gently fold into batter. Bake on a hot waffle iron 3–5 minutes until golden brown.

Pizza Dough

Easy

Yield: 14 inch pan
Preparation time:
  10–15 minutes
Bake 20 minutes

This is a quick, easy pizza dough that even kids can make.

1 cup warm water
1 pkg. yeast
1 tsp. sugar
1 tsp. salt
2 Tbsp. Crisco® oil
$2^1/_2$ cups flour

Preheat oven to 400°. Sprinkle yeast on warm water, then stir it in. Add sugar to the yeast water; wait until bubbles form. In a large bowl, combine yeast, water, salt and oil. Mix in flour and stir 20 seconds, or mix in food processor until a ball forms. Allow dough to "rest" about 7 minutes. Spread in a greased pizza pan. Add your favorite sauce, toppings and cheese. Bake at 400° for 20 minutes.

Sour Cream Pancakes

1   cup flour
1   cup milk
1   cup sour cream
2   eggs
1   Tbsp. sugar
$^1/_4$ tsp. salt
$^1/_2$ tsp. baking soda

Mix all ingredients together; beat until smooth. Pour batter into a hot, greased skillet. Flip when the bubbles appear.

Easy

Yield: 20 pancakes
Preparation time:
* 10 minutes*
Cook 2–3 minutes

Light non-filling pancakes

Apple Muffins

Easy

Yield: 24 muffins
Preparation time:
 15 minutes
Bake 25 minutes

*Great for breakfast.
If you don't have
muffin tins, you can
buy muffin papers
with a foil layer and
place them on a
cookie sheet.*

4	cups diced apple with skins
1	cup sugar
2	eggs, beaten
$\frac{1}{2}$	cup Crisco® oil
2	tsp. vanilla extract
2	cups all purpose flour
2	tsp. baking soda
2	tsp. cinnamon
1	tsp. salt
1	cup raisins
1	cup broken walnuts

Preheat oven to 325°. Put apples and sugar in a bowl. In a second bowl, mix eggs, oil, and vanilla extract. In a third bowl, mix remainder of ingredients. Stir the egg mixture into the apple mixture. Sprinkle with flour mixture, mix thoroughly. Bake at 325° for 25 minutes.

Banana Muffins

$^1/_2$	cup shortening of your choice (butter, margarine, Crisco®), softened
$^1/_2$	cup sugar
2	beaten eggs
2	cups flour, sifted
$^1/_2$	tsp. salt
1	tsp. baking powder
$^3/_4$	tsp. baking soda
$^1/_4$	cup sour milk (Milk may be soured by combining $^1/_4$ cup less $^2/_3$ Tbsp. milk with $^2/_3$ Tbsp. vinegar and waiting 10 minutes.)
1	cup mashed bananas, put through a sieve
1	tsp. vanilla

Easy

Yield: 2$^1/_2$ dozen
Preparation time:
 10 minutes
Bake 20 minutes

Freezes well

A very light muffin.

Preheat oven to 375°. Thoroughly cream shortening and sugar until smooth. Add eggs and beat well with mixer. Sift together dry ingredients. Add sifted ingredients alternately with sour milk, bananas and vanilla. Stir well. Fill greased cupcake pan (or use paper fillers) half full. Bake at 375° for 20 minutes.

Blueberry Muffins

Easy

Yield: 12–15
 muffins
Preparation time:
 10 minutes
Bake 25–30 minutes

Freezes well

*For lemony blue-
berry muffins, toss
blueberries with 2
tsp. grated lemon
rind.*

1   cup sugar
2   cups flour
2$\frac{1}{2}$ tsp. baking powder
$\frac{1}{2}$ cup margarine
1   16 oz. pkg. frozen blueberries, thawed
2   eggs
$\frac{1}{2}$ cup milk
1   tsp. vanilla
Sugar to sprinkle on top
Muffin papers

Preheat to 375°. Mix dry ingredients in large bowl. Cut in margarine with pastry blender (you can also use a mixer); mix thoroughly. Rinse and drain blueberries. Add to flour. Mix together eggs, milk and vanilla. Add to flour and blueberries, being careful not to over-stir or crush berries. Spoon into paper-lined muffin tins. Sprinkle top with sugar. Bake at 375° for 30 minutes. Cool on a rack.

Carrot-Wheat Muffins

$^3/_4$ cup whole wheat flour
2   tsp. baking powder
$^1/_2$ tsp. pumpkin pie spice
2   Tbsp. wheat germ
1   cup grated carrots
$^1/_2$ cup raisins
1   egg, slightly beaten
1   cup milk
$^1/_4$ cup honey
$^1/_4$ cup Crisco® oil
$1^1/_2$ cups shredded wheat and bran cereal

Moderate

Yield: 1 dozen
Preparation time:
* 20–25 minutes*
Bake 18–20 minutes

Freezes well

Preheat oven to 400°. Combine the first 6 ingredients in a medium bowl; set aside. Combine egg and remaining ingredients in a small bowl. Stir well and let stand 3–5 minutes. Make a well in the center of the flour mixture. Add cereal mixture to the dry ingredients, stirring just until moistened. Spoon into greased muffin pans, filling $^3/_4$ full. Bake at 400° for 18–20 minutes.

Orange Muffins

1	cup sugar
2	oranges, zest and juice
1	cup butter
2	eggs
1	tsp. baking soda
1	cup buttermilk
2	cups flour
$\frac{1}{2}$	cup golden raisins
1	cup brown sugar

Place sugar and orange zest in a work bowl of food processor. Process until finely chopped. Add butter, cream well. Add eggs, mix well. Dissolve the soda in buttermilk and allow to sit a few minutes. Add to mixing bowl; process briefly. Add flour and raisins and mix only until flour disappears. (Use on-off motion.) Fill greased muffin tins ²/₃ full. Bake in a preheated oven, 15–20 minutes at 400°. Mix orange juice and brown sugar. As soon as they come out of the oven, prick muffins with a toothpick all over and spoon juice mixture over them.

Desserts

Apricot Nectar Cake

Cake:
1   yellow cake mix (not pudding cake mix)
4   eggs
$^{1}/_{2}$ cup sugar
$^{1}/_{2}$ cup Crisco® oil
1   cup apricot nectar

Glaze:
1   cup sugar
$^{1}/_{2}$ cup buttermilk
$^{1}/_{2}$ tsp. soda
$^{1}/_{2}$ tsp. vanilla
$^{1}/_{2}$ cup margarine

Cake:
Mix all ingredients for 4 minutes. Pour into greased and floured tube pan. Bake for 50 minutes at 350°.

Glaze:
Combine all ingredients in saucepan. Boil 1 minute without stirring. Poke holes in cake. Pour glaze over cake.

Easy

Serves 8–12
May prepare ahead
Preparation time:
30 minutes
Bake 50 minutes

Chocolate Sheik Cake

Easy

Serves 12
May prepare ahead
Preparation time:
 10 minutes
Bake 20 minutes

Cake:
1   tsp. baking soda
$^1/_2$ cup buttermilk
1   cup water
4   Tbsp. cocoa powder
2   sticks margarine
2   cups all-purpose flour
2   cups sugar
$^1/_4$ tsp. salt
2   eggs
2   tsp. vanilla

Frosting:
1   stick margarine
4   Tbsp. cocoa powder
6   Tbsp. milk
1   lb. sifted powdered sugar
1   cup chopped pecans
1   tsp. vanilla

Cake:

Mix soda and buttermilk and let sit. Combine water, cocoa, and margarine in saucepan. Bring to a boil, stirring when it just begins to boil. While waiting for boil, sift flour, sugar, and salt together three times in large bowl. Remove boiling mixture and stir this into the dry ingredients. Add buttermilk mixture. Add eggs, one at a time, beating well. Add vanilla. Bake in greased 13x9x2 pan or two 8x8 pans for 20 minutes at 375°. Frost cake while it is still hot.

Frosting:
In saucepan, bring margarine, cocoa, and milk to a boil. Remove from heat. Add powdered sugar, pecans, and vanilla. Pour over warm cake. Leave cake in pan and cut from the pan.

Flower Garden Cake

6	eggs
³/₄	cup sugar
³/₄	cup fresh lemon juice
1¹/₂	tsp. grated lemon peel
1	Tbsp. unflavored gelatin
¹/₄	cup cold water
³/₄	cup sugar
1	large round angel food cake

Moderate

Serves 8–10
Prepare ahead
Preparation time:
 20 minutes
Chill 3 hours

A light lemon cake

Separate eggs; beat egg yolks. Using a double boiler, make a custard of egg yolks, sugar, lemon juice, and lemon peel over boiling water. Cook until mixture coats spoon; remove from heat. Soak gelatin in cold water; add to custard. Combine egg whites and sugar; beat until stiff. Fold into custard mixture. Tear cake into bite-sized pieces. Place a layer of cake pieces in an oiled tube or spring pan (use vegetable oil). Pour ¹/₂ custard over cake layer. Add remaining cake and custard in layers; mix cake/custard with a fork. Chill until firm (about 3 hours). Serve with whipped cream; garnish with fresh mint leaves.

Fresh Apple Cake

Easy

Serves 8-12
Prepare ahead
Preparation time:
 20 minutes
Bake 1 hour and
 10 minutes

Great fall dessert

Cake:
1	cup Crisco® oil
2	cups sugar
2	eggs
3	cups (2 large) apples, chopped, but not peeled
3	cups flour
1/2	tsp. salt
1 1/2	tsp. soda
1	tsp. vanilla
1	cup chopped walnuts or pecans

Icing:
1	cup powdered sugar
Juice of 1 lemon	
1/4	tsp. salt

Cake:
Mix all ingredients well. Bake in stem, loaf or bundt pan for 1 hour and 10 minutes in 350° oven. Ice while still warm.

Icing:
Mix all ingredients well. Pour over warm cake.

Hot Gingerbread

$^{1}/_{2}$ cup Crisco®
$^{1}/_{2}$ cup sugar
1   egg
1   cup light molasses
1   cup hot water
2$^{1}/_{2}$ cups flour
$^{1}/_{2}$ tsp. salt
1$^{1}/_{2}$ tsp. soda
1   tsp. cinnamon
1   tsp. ginger
$^{1}/_{2}$ tsp. cloves

Easy

Serves 12
Prepare ahead
Preparation time:
  15 minutes
Bake 50–60 minutes

Thoroughly cream shortening and sugar. Add egg; beat well. Combine molasses and hot water. Sift dry ingredients together. Add molasses mixture alternately with dry ingredients to shortening and egg mixture. Pour into well-greased pan (9x9 or 9x12). Bake at 350° for 50–60 minutes.

Oreo® Cheesecake

Moderate

Serves 12
Prepare ahead
Preparation time:
 1 hour
Bake 1 hour
 15 minutes

Chill overnight

Crust:
1¼ cups graham cracker crumbs
⅓ cup unsalted butter, melted
¼ cup firmly packed light brown sugar
1 tsp. cinnamon

Filling:
2 lb. cream cheese, room temperature
1½ cups sugar
2 tsp. flour
6 eggs
3 egg yolks
⅓ cup whipping cream
2 tsp. vanilla
1½ cups chopped Oreo® cookies
2 cups sour cream

Glaze:
1 cup whipping cream
8 oz. semi-sweet chocolate
1 tsp. vanilla

Crust:
Blend all ingredients in bottom of a 10-inch springform pan, then press into bottom and sides. Refrigerate until firm, about 30 minutes.

Filling:
Preheat oven to 425°. Beat cream cheese in large bowl on low speed until smooth. Beat in 1¼ cups sugar and flour until well blended.

Beat in eggs and yolks until mixture is smooth. Stir in cream and 1 tsp. vanilla. Pour half the batter into prepared crust. Sprinkle with chopped Oreos®. Pour remaining batter over, smoothing with spatula. Bake 15 minutes. Reduce oven temperature to 225°; bake 50 minutes, covering loosely with foil if browning too quickly. Increase oven temperature to 350°. Blend sour cream, remaining $\frac{1}{4}$ cup sugar and remaining 1 tsp. vanilla in small bowl. Spread over cake. Bake 7 minutes. Refrigerate immediately. Cover cake with plastic wrap and chill overnight.

Glaze:
Scald cream in heavy saucepan over medium heat. Add chocolate and vanilla and stir until all chocolate is melted. Refrigerate 10 minutes. Set cake on platter and remove springform. Pour glaze over top of cake. Refrigerate until ready to serve.

Kahlua Cake

Easy

*Serves 12-15
Preparation time:
  15-20 minutes
Bake 50-60 minutes*

Freezes well

*Commonly
requested*

Cake:
1   pkg. white cake mix
1   3 oz. pkg. instant chocolate pudding
4   eggs
1   cup Crisco® oil
²/₃ cup vodka
¹/₃ cup Kahlua
¹/₄ cup water

Glaze:
¹/₄ cup Kahlua
¹/₂ cup confectioners sugar

Cake:
Combine all ingredients. Beat 5 minutes. Pour into greased and floured bundt pan. Bake at 350° for 50-60 minutes until tester comes out clean. Cool 5 minutes in pan; invert onto rack. Glaze while still warm.

Glaze:
Mix ingredients well; drizzle over cake.

Pineapple Cake

Cake:

2	cups sugar
2	sticks margarine
5	eggs
1	tsp. vanilla
2½	cups graham cracker crumbs
2	tsp. baking powder
1	cup nuts
1	cup crushed pineapple (well drained)
1	cup coconut

Icing:

1	box confectioner's sugar
1	stick margarine (soft or melted)
1	cup pineapple (well drained)

Coconut (optional)
Nuts (optional)

Easy

Serves 12
Prepare ahead
Preparation time:
 20 minutes
Bake 30 minutes

Cake:
Beat together sugar and margarine. Add eggs one at a time. Mix in vanilla, graham cracker crumbs and baking powder. Fold in nuts, pineapple and coconut. Pour into 9x13 pan. Bake at 350° for 30 minutes. Ice when cool.

Icing:
Mix all ingredients, including coconut if desired. Nuts may be sprinkled on top.

Pineapple-Banana Torte

Moderate

Serves 9
Prepare ahead
Preparation time:
30 minutes
Chill 24 hours

Great for parties!

1 stick unsalted butter, softened
1½ cups confectioner's sugar
2 eggs
1 cup graham cracker crumbs
1 large can crushed pineapple, drained well
3 bananas, sliced
½ pint whipping cream
2 Tbsp. sugar
Dash of vanilla

Cream butter and sugar. Add eggs, beat well. Line 8x8 pan with ½ graham cracker crumbs. Spread the egg and sugar mixture over this, then the pineapple. Layer sliced banana on top of the pineapple. Whip the cream with sugar and vanilla. Spread on top of the bananas. Sprinkle the remaining crumbs over the top. Refrigerate overnight.

Strawberry Cake

Cake:
1   3 oz. pkg. strawberry gelatin
¹/₂   cup water
1   pkg. white cake mix
4   eggs
1   cup Crisco® oil
¹/₂   cup juice from 10 oz. package of frozen strawberries (thawed)

Icing
¹/₂   stick butter
1   box confectioner's sugar
Drained strawberries from 10 oz. package

Easy

Serves 12-15
Prepare ahead
Preparation time:
 15 minutes
Bake 30 minutes

Freezes well

A very moist cake;
great in spring and
summer

Cake:
Soften gelatin in ¹/₂ cup water. Combine with other ingredients and blend together with electric mixer at least 4 minutes. Bake in three 9-inch pans or one 13x9 pan at 350° for 30 minutes, or until tester comes out clean. Cool before icing.

Icing:
Cream together butter and sugar. Add as much of the drained strawberries as mixture will take and still spread well. Frost cake and serve.

Heath Bar Crunch

Easy

Prepare ahead
Preparation time:
 30 minutes

Chill 1 hour

1   box saltine crackers
1   cup butter
1   cup dark brown sugar
1   12 oz. pkg. chocolate chips
$\frac{1}{2}$ 12 oz. pkg. Bits of Brickle®

Cover cookie sheet with foil, then grease with butter. Bring butter and brown sugar to a boil in a saucepan and then simmer for 5 minutes. Put a layer of saltines on cookie sheet close together. Pour boiled mixture over crackers and bake 10 minutes. Immediately pour chocolate chips over crackers, spreading as they melt. Sprinkle on brickle bits. Chill in refrigerator, then break into bits.

Old Fashioned Fudge

$^2/_3$ cup Hershey's® cocoa
3   cups sugar
Dash salt
$1^1/_2$ cups milk
4   Tbsp. butter
1   tsp. vanilla
Nuts, optional

Moderate

Yield: 1$^1/_2$ lb.
Preparation time:
1 hour

*Tastes as good as
you remember it did*

Combine cocoa, sugar and salt. Stir in part of the milk to dampen dry ingredients, then stir in rest. Boil, stirring occasionally, until a drop of syrup dropped into cold water forms a soft ball. (It keeps its shape as you lift it with your finger, but does not feel firm.) Remove from heat and add butter and vanilla. Let cool. When fudge is cool enough to touch, beat with a spoon until fudge loses its gloss. Quickly add nuts, then pour onto buttered platter. Cool until firm. It should firm up without refrigeration. Cut into squares.

Aunt Mimi's Lace Cookies

Moderate

Yield: 2–3 dozen
May prepare ahead
Preparation time:
 1 hour 15 minutes
Bake 8 minutes

These crisp and delicate cookies are best attempted on a cool dry day.

Serve with crème brulée, gingered fresh fruit, or ice cream.

1 cup sugar
1 cup oatmeal (minute or instant)
3 Tbsp. all purpose flour
$^1/_4$ tsp. salt
$^1/_2$ tsp. baking powder
$^1/_2$ cup butter, melted (do not substitute margarine)
2 tsp. vanilla
1 whole egg, beaten

Mix all dry ingredients. Add butter, vanilla and egg; mix well. Refrigerate 1 hour (or freeze 20 minutes). Cover cookie sheet with tin foil (do not grease). Preheat oven to 350°. Drop $^1/_4$ tsp. to $^1/_2$ tsp. of dough per cookie on cookie sheet, allowing plenty of room for spreading. Bake 8 minutes, watching carefully to avoid burning. Cool slightly until cookies easily peel off. Cooling tins outside your back door for a few minutes on a cold day speeds up total preparation time and makes removal easier. Store in airtight container.

Chinese Almond Cookies

1 cup butter, softened
1 cup sugar
2 eggs
1 Tbsp. almond extract
2¹/₂ cups flour
¹/₂ tsp. salt
Whole blanched almonds

Moderate

Yield: 2–3 dozen
May prepare ahead
Preparation time:
 30 minutes
Bake 10 minutes

Beat butter. Cream butter, sugar, 1 egg and almond extract. Beat in flour and salt. Make 1 inch balls from dough and place 2 inches apart on ungreased cookie sheet. Flatten balls slightly with heel of hand. Place 1 almond on top of each cookie. Mix remaining egg with 1 Tbsp. water. Brush egg mixture on cookies before and after baking. Bake at 375° for 10–12 minutes.

Bourbon Brownies

Moderate

Serves 30
Prepare ahead
Preparation time:
 20 minutes
Bake 25 minutes
Chill 30 minutes

Brownies:
2	Tbsp. water
$\frac{1}{2}$	cup sugar
$\frac{1}{3}$	cup margarine
1	6 oz. pkg. chocolate chips
$\frac{1}{2}$	tsp. vanilla
2	eggs
$\frac{3}{4}$	cup flour
$\frac{1}{4}$	tsp. salt
$\frac{1}{4}$	tsp. baking powder
1	cup chopped nuts
4	tsp. bourbon

Frosting:
$\frac{1}{2}$	cup softened margarine
2	cups confectioners sugar
7	tsp. green creme de menthe
1	6 oz. pkg. chocolate chips
3	Tbsp. Crisco® shortening

Brownies:
Combine water, sugar, and margarine in a saucepan; bring to a boil, stirring constantly. Remove from heat and stir in chocolate chips and vanilla. Beat until smooth, then beat in eggs, then flour, salt and baking powder. Add nuts. Spread into a greased 9x13 pan. Bake at 325° for 25 minutes. Remove from oven and sprinkle bourbon over hot brownies. Cool thoroughly, then frost.

Frosting:
Cream margarine and sugar, then blend in creme de menthe. Spread over brownies and chill until set. Then melt chocolate chips and Crisco® together and drizzle over mint layer. When chocolate sets, cut into small squares. Keep refrigerated.

Chocolate-Dipped Pecan Cookies

1½ sticks butter, softened
⅓ cup sugar
2 cups flour
1½ cups ground pecans (about 6 oz.)
¼ tsp. vanilla
12 oz. semi-sweet chocolate chips
⅛ bar paraffin

Moderate

Yield: 3–4 dozen
May prepare ahead
Preparation time:
30 minutes
Bake 10 minutes

Freezes well

Cream butter and sugar until light and fluffy. Add flour, nuts and vanilla, and stir until dough forms a ball. Shape dough into two flat rounds, wrap in plastic wrap and refrigerate until firm enough to roll. Preheat oven to 350°. Roll dough ⅛ inch thick and cut into shapes. Bake on cookie sheets 10 minutes until golden. Cool completely. Melt chocolate with paraffin in double boiler. Dip each cookie so ½ is covered with chocolate. Place on waxed paper until chocolate sets. Store in airtight tins.

Chocolate Mint Bars

Easy

Yield: 16 bars
May prepare ahead
Preparation time:
 20 minutes
Bake 25 minutes
Chill 45 minutes

Freezes well

Decadently delicious

First layer:
$^3/_4$ cup sugar
1   stick butter
3   eggs, beaten
1   cup flour
$^1/_2$ tsp. salt
1   16 oz. can chocolate syrup

Second layer:
2   cups powdered sugar
1   stick butter
2   Tbsp. milk
1   scant tsp. peppermint
4–5 drops green food coloring

Third layer:
1   cup chocolate chips
6   Tbsp. butter

First layer:
Cream sugar and butter. Add eggs, flour, and salt. Add chocolate syrup. Bake in a 9x13 pan at 350° for 20–25 minutes. Cool.

Second layer:
Mix powdered sugar, butter and milk. Add peppermint and food coloring. Spread over first layer and chill 30 minutes.

Third layer:
Melt chocolate chips and butter. Drizzle over second layer and refrigerate until glazed. Cut into bars.

Congo Squares

2 cups flour
¹/₄ tsp. baking soda
1 tsp. baking powder
1 tsp. salt
1 cup chopped pecans
²/₃ cup margarine
2 cups brown sugar, packed
2 eggs, slightly beaten
2 tsp. vanilla
1 6 oz. pkg. chocolate chips

Easy

Serves 16
Prepare ahead
Preparation time:
 15 minutes
Bake 30 minutes

Mix flour, soda, baking powder, and salt. Add pecans. Melt margarine in saucepan. Remove from heat. Mix brown sugar with margarine. Cool. Stir eggs and vanilla into margarine/sugar mixture. Add flour mixture, gradually. Mix well. Add ³/₄ package chocolate chips to mixture. Pour into greased 13x9x2 pan. Sprinkle remaining chocolate chips on top. Bake at 350° for 30 minutes. Cool. Cut into bars.

Elegant Kahlua Bars

Bars:
1½ cups graham cracker crumbs
1 cup chopped, toasted almonds
½ cup butter
¼ cup sugar
½ cup cocoa
1 egg, slightly beaten
1½ tsp. vanilla
3 Tbsp. Kahlua

Icing:
6 Tbsp. unsalted butter, softened
1¾ cups confectioner's sugar
1 Tbsp. cream or milk
3 Tbsp. Kahlua

Topping:
1½ Tbsp. butter
4 oz. semisweet chocolate

Bars:
Combine cracker crumbs and almonds in a large bowl. Melt butter in small saucepan over low heat. Add sugar, cocoa, egg, and vanilla. Cook slowly for 4 minutes or until thickened. Pour over crumb mixture and toss gently. Sprinkle Kahlua over mixture; mix gently. Press into 7x11 pan. Place in freezer.

Icing:
Beat together butter and confectioner's sugar in medium bowl. Add cream and Kahlua; mix well. Spread over bar layer; freeze 2 hours.

Topping:
Melt butter and chocolate in small saucepan over low heat. Spread over icing. Cut into bars and put back in freezer. Remove from freezer 30 minutes before serving.

Madeleines

3/4 cup sugar
1/2 cup flour
1 1/2 sticks butter, melted
1 tsp. vanilla or rum flavoring
2 eggs

Easy

Yield: 12 madeleines
May prepare ahead
Preparation time:
 10 minutes
Bake 10 minutes

Blend all ingredients well. Pour into well-greased madeleine pans, filling halfway. Bake at 350° for 10–12 minutes, until lightly browned.

These can be dipped halfway in chocolate or sprinkled with powdered sugar.

Sugar Cookies

Easy

Yield: 4–5 dozen
Prepare ahead
Preparation time:
30 minutes
Chill overnight
Bake 8 minutes

$1\frac{1}{2}$ cups confectioner's sugar, sifted
2 sticks butter
1 egg
1 tsp. vanilla
$\frac{1}{2}$ tsp. almond extract
$2\frac{1}{2}$ cups flour
1 tsp. cream of tartar
1 tsp. baking soda

Cream together sugar and butter. Add egg and vanilla and almond extract. In another bowl, mix together flour, cream of tartar and baking soda. Add flour mixture to sugar mixture. Form dough into ball. Cover with wax paper. Chill overnight. Roll out, cut with cookie cutters. Bake at 350° for 8 minutes on buttered baking sheet.

Yorkshire Butter Cookies

1 stick ($^1/_2$ cup) butter
$^1/_2$ cup sugar
1 cup flour
1 egg yolk
1 tsp. vanilla
Pinch salt
Raspberry preserves

Soften butter to room temperature. Mix sugar, flour, egg yolk, vanilla, and salt into butter. Pinch off small pieces and roll into 1" balls. Place balls on ungreased cookie sheet. Press thumbprint into center of each and fill with preserves. Bake at 350° for 15–20 minutes.

Easy

Yield: 2 dozen
Prepare ahead
Preparation time:
 15 minutes
Bake 15–20 minutes

Great for teas or receptions. Never-fail recipe!

Frozen Apricot Bombe
with Mocha Sauce

Moderate

Serves 10–12
Prepare ahead
Preparation time:
 20 minutes
Freeze overnight

Freezes well

Fresh strawberries
make a wonderful
garnish

Mocha sauce:
1   12 oz. pkg. semi-sweet chocolate chunks
2   squares (2 oz.) unsweetened chocolate
1   12 oz. can evaporated milk
1   Tbsp. strong instant coffee
1   tsp. pure vanilla

Bombe:
$^3/_4$ cup apricot brandy
25   marshmallows
$^1/_2$ cup chopped apricots
2   tsp. grated lemon rind
1   pint whipped cream
Fresh strawberries for garnish, if desired

Mocha Sauce:
Heat water in double boiler to boiling. In top of double boiler: melt chocolate chunks and squares; add coffee and milk, $^1/_4$ cup at a time; mix well. Remove from heat and stir in vanilla. Set aside; reheat when ready to serve bombe.

Bombe:
Line a 1-quart mold with plastic wrap. In top of double boiler, combine brandy and marshmallows. When liquid, remove from heat and cool to room temperature. Fold in chopped apricots and lemon rind, blend well. Fold in whipped cream; pour into mold. Freeze overnight. Remove from freezer 15 minutes before serving; pour mocha sauce over bombe and garnish with strawberries.

Nectarine Frozen Yogurt Creme

3	medium-sized fresh nectarines, chopped
1	cup sugar
2	egg whites
1	Tbsp. lemon juice
1	cup whipping cream
$\frac{1}{2}$	cup plain yogurt

Combine nectarines, sugar, egg whites and lemon juice in large mixing bowl. Beat with high speed until very fluffy and stiff, approximately 7 minutes. Whip cream in separate bowl until stiff peaks form. Fold whipped cream and yogurt into nectarine mixture. Turn into plastic freezer container.   Cover and freeze overnight. Scoop into dessert dishes.

Easy

Serves 8
May prepare ahead
Preparation time:
 15 minutes
Freeze overnight

Garnish with nectarine wedges and mint sprigs

Frozen Lemon Soufflé with Raspberry Sauce

Moderate

Serves 8
Prepare ahead
Preparation time:
1 hour
Freeze overnight

Freezes well

$^1/_2$ gallon Breyer's® vanilla ice cream with lemon sorbet

8 crumbled macaroon cookies

$^3/_4$ cup lemon juice

2 cups whipping cream

$^1/_4$ cup slivered almonds

$^1/_2$ cup sifted powdered sugar

Soften ice cream and stir in macaroons. Stir in lemon juice. Whip whipping cream until stiff peaks form. Add cream to ice cream mixture and fold together. Pour into a 10" springform pan. Sprinkle top with almonds and powdered sugar. Cover and freeze overnight. Let sit out about 10 minutes before serving. Loosen edge of pan and turn out onto a serving plate. To serve: spoon raspberry sauce on a plate and top with slice of lemon soufflé.

Raspberry Sauce
for Lemon Soufflé

1 pint fresh raspberries
Juice from half a lemon
$1/_4$ cup water
$1/_2$ cup sugar
$1/_2$ tsp. cornstarch

Moderate

Serves 8
Prepare ahead
Preparation time:
* 30 minutes*
Chill at least
* 20 minutes*

Combine raspberries, lemon juice, and water in food processor. Purée until smooth. Strain through a sieve to remove some seeds. Pour mixture into a saucepan. Add sugar. Bring to boil over medium-high heat. Simmer 15 minutes. Dissolve cornstarch into a little cold water. Stir into raspberry mixture. Remove from heat. Cool. Refrigerate until ready to serve.

Sabra Ice Cream Pie

Easy

Serves 10–12
Prepare ahead
Preparation time:
 20 minutes
Chill 2–3 hours

Freezes well

Decorate with
chocolate curls

1½ cups chocolate wafer crumbs
½ cup butter
1 envelope unflavored gelatin
¼ cup water
½ cup plus 2 Tbsp. Sabra (Israeli liqueur)
1 pint softened chocolate ice cream
1 cup heavy cream

Combine chocolate wafer crumbs and butter, press into 9" pan. Bake at 375° for 8 minutes. Soften gelatin in water in small saucepan. Add ½ cup Sabra, heat until mixture is clear. Stir into chocolate ice cream. Whip heavy cream with 2 Tbsp. Sabra. Fold into ice cream mixture and spoon into crust. Chill or freeze until set.

Sorbet

Easy

Yield varies
Preparation time:
 10 minutes

Fresh fruit
Sugar, Karo® syrup or honey

Put fruit in blender. Add sugar, Karo® or honey to desired sweetness. Add ice to obtain mushy consistency. Put in parfait glasses, champagne glasses, etc.

Tortoni

1   tsp. vanilla
1   Tbsp. light rum
1   cup chilled whipping cream
2   Tbsp. powdered sugar
$1/_3$ cup chopped macaroons
$1/_4$ cup chopped toasted almonds

Place vanilla and rum into a large bowl. Beat the whipping cream into the vanilla and rum, adding sugar gradually until soft peaks form. Fold in the macaroons and spoon the mixture into 4 paper-lined foil muffin cups. Sprinkle with almonds. Freeze until firm, at least 2 hours. When ready to serve, place cup into a pretty glass dish. Let sit out 5 minutes before serving.

Moderate

Serves 4
Prepare ahead
Preparation time:
20 minutes
Freeze at least
2 hours

Freezes well

Perfect after any
Italian dinner.

Broiled Pears
with Chocolate Sauce

Moderate

Serves 8
Partially prepare
ahead
Preparation time:
20 minutes
Broil 5 minutes

Chocolate Sauce:
1½ cups sugar
⅛   tsp. salt
⅛   tsp. cream of tartar
9   Tbsp. cocoa or 3 oz. melted
     bitter chocolate
1   13½ oz. can evaporated milk
1   Tbsp. butter
1   tsp. vanilla

Pears:
4   large ripe pears
1   lemon, halved
2   Tbsp. butter, melted
Sugar
Mint, pear, or apple leaves for garnish

Chocolate Sauce:
Mix sugar, salt, cream of tartar, and cocoa.
Add evaporated milk. Cook in saucepan over
low heat, stirring constantly until it comes to a
rolling boil. Remove from heat; stir in butter
and vanilla.

Pears:
Preheat broiler. Line baking sheet with foil;
lightly butter foil. Peel pears. Halve lengthwise and remove cores. Immediately rub with
lemon to prevent discoloration. Using a sharp
knife, score rounded side of pears lengthwise;
do not cut through. Arrange pears round side
up on prepared sheet. Brush with melted

butter. Sprinkle generously with sugar. Broil 4 inches from heat until golden brown, about 5 minutes. Spoon chocolate sauce onto dessert plates. Top with pears. Garnish with mint leaves, or with pear or apple leaves if available. Serve immediately.

Strawberries Royale

1–1 $^{1}/_{2}$ quarts fresh strawberries
$^{1}/_{4}$ cup Kirsch
1   10 oz. pkg. frozen raspberries, thawed
$^{1}/_{2}$ pint whipping cream or $^{1}/_{2}$ pint sour cream
1   Tbsp. brown sugar

Easy

Serves 8
Prepare ahead
Preparation time:
  15 minutes
Chill at least two
  hours

Light and elegant

Wash, hull, and slice or quarter strawberries. Toss strawberries with Kirsch in bowl. Purée raspberries with their juice in blender. Pour purée over strawberries. Toss lightly to mix. Refrigerate at least 2 hours. Mix sour cream and brown sugar, or whipped cream, and top dessert. Serve in sherbet or parfait glasses.

Coffee Pudding

Moderate

Serves 6
Prepare ahead
Preparation time:
 30 minutes
Chill at least 4 hours

This is an elegant,
mousse-like dessert

24   marshmallows

$^3/_4$ cup very strong coffee (may use instant
        mixed with water)

$^3/_4$ pint heavy whipping cream

3   Tbsp. creme de cacao

Shaved or grated semi-sweet chocolate

Place water in bottom of double boiler. Replace top and bring to a boil. Place marshmallows and coffee in top of double boiler. Heat until marshmallows are melted. Stir well and cool to room temperature. Whip cream until very stiff, without becoming butter, or coffee will separate and go to the bottom of serving container. Pour cream into cooled mixture. Stir in creme de cacao. Place in champagne glasses for individual servings, or in an attractive glass bowl. Garnish with grated chocolate. Chill at least 4 hours. May be made a day ahead.

Molded Spirits

1 Tbsp. unflavored gelatin
1 cup water
$^1/_3$ cup sugar
$^1/_2$ cup orange juice
$^1/_2$ cup bourbon
Whipped cream and nutmeg for garnish

Easy

Serves 4
May prepare ahead
Preparation time:
  15 minutes
Chill several hours

Mysterious and light

Sprinkle gelatin over $^1/_4$ cup water. Boil remaining water and pour over softened gelatin, stirring until dissolved. Stir in sugar and let dissolve. Stir in orange juice and bourbon. Pour into individual molds and chill until set. Serve garnished with whipped cream topped with a light sprinkle of nutmeg. For a variation, in place of bourbon, use $^3/_4$ cup cream sherry, 1 tablespoon lemon juice, and a dash of salt. Garnish with whipped cream and sliced fresh strawberries.

Chocolate Angel Pie

Moderate

Serves 12
May prepare ahead
Preparation time:
 30 minutes
Bake 1 hour
Chill 2–3 hours

Pie Shell:
3   egg whites
$^1/_4$ teaspoon cream of tartar
Dash of salt
$^3/_4$ cup sugar

Pie Filling:
$^2/_3$ cup butter
1   cup sugar
3   whole eggs
3   squares (3 oz.) bitter chocolate
$^1/_3$ cup chocolate chips

Pie Shell:
Beat egg whites until stiff, but not dry. Gradually add cream of tartar, salt and sugar and continue beating until stiff and satiny. Spread $^2/_3$ of mixture on the bottom and sides of a well-greased 8" pie pan. Drop remaining meringue in mounds around the rim of the pan. Bake for 1 hour at 275° until the shell is lightly browned and crisp. Cool.

Pie Filling:
Cream butter and sugar until light and fluffy, about 10–15 minutes. Add eggs one at a time, beating after each addition. Melt chocolate and chocolate chips and add to mixture. Beat until very thick. Pour into pie shell and refrigerate 2–3 hours.

Chocolate French Silk Pie

1½ sticks butter
1½ oz. bitter chocolate
¾ cup sugar
2 unbeaten eggs
1 tsp. vanilla
8" baked pie crust
Whipped cream

Easy

Serves 8
Prepare ahead
Preparation time:
  30 minutes
Chill 4 hours or
  overnight

A chocolate lover's
delight

Melt and cool chocolate. Using electric mixer at medium speed, cream butter and add sugar gradually, creaming the mixture. Blend in melted and cooled chocolate. Add vanilla. Add eggs, one at a time, beating 5 minutes after each addition (you must beat as directed). Pour into prepared pie crust. Chill 4 hours or overnight. Top with whipped cream.

Chocolate Meringue Pie

Easy

Serves 8–10
May prepare ahead
Preparation time:
15 minutes
Bake 1 hour
Set 2 hours
Chill 2 hours

Meringue crust:
4–5 egg whites (reserve 3 yolks for filling)
1   tsp. vinegar
$\frac{1}{2}$ tsp. cinnamon or more to taste
$\frac{1}{4}$ tsp. salt
$\frac{3}{4}$ cup sugar

Filling:
6   oz. semi-sweet chocolate or
     chocolate bits
$\frac{1}{4}$ cup water
3   egg yolks

Topping:
1   pint whipping cream
$\frac{1}{4}$ cup sugar
$\frac{1}{2}$ tsp. cinnamon
Chocolate shavings

Meringue crust:
Grease pie plate and preheat oven to 275°. Whip with mixer until stiff the egg whites, vinegar, cinnamon and salt, adding sugar gradually. Bake at 275° on middle rack for one hour. Turn off oven; leave in oven two more hours to dry out. Cool.

Filling:
Melt chocolate with water. Beat egg yolks with fork; add to chocolate. Remove from heat and chill until thick. Spread 2 Tbsp. filling onto cooled pie crust.

Topping:

Whip cream, sugar and cinnamon. Mix one third of whipped cream into remaining chocolate filling and spread on pie crust. Top with remaining two thirds whipped cream and sprinkle with chocolate shavings. Chill at least two hours in refrigerator.

Gold Lattice Key Lime Pie

Moderate

Serves 8–10
Prepare ahead
Preparation time:
 1 hour 15 minutes
Bake 10–15 minutes

Crust
Your favorite pie crust dough
1   tsp. grated lime peel
2   Tbsp. sugar
2–3 Tbsp. key or regular lime juice

Graham Cracker Crunch:
1   cup graham cracker crumbs
1/4   cup sugar
1/4   cup butter-flavored shortening, melted

Filling:
2   14 oz. cans sweetened condensed milk
3   egg yolks
1/2   cup plain low-fat yogurt
1 1/2 tsp. grated key lime peel
2/3   cup key lime juice or regular lime juice

Meringue:
3   egg whites
1   tsp. lime juice
6   Tbsp. sugar

Gold Lattice:
1   cup sugar

Crust:
To your favorite pie crust recipe, add lime peel
and sugar to flour, and replace liquid with lime
juice. Place dough on lightly floured wax
paper. Roll crust 1 inch larger than inverted
10" pie plate. Gently lift dough into the plate.

314

Trim to $1/2$ inch beyond the edge. Flute edges and prick bottom all over with fork.

Graham Cracker Crunch:
Combine ingredients in bowl and set aside. Bake pie crust for 12–18 minutes in a 400° oven. Remove from oven. While hot, sprinkle bottom of crust evenly with half the graham cracker mixture. Reserve the other half for filling.

Filling:
Combine milk, egg yolks, yogurt, lime peel and juice. Stir until smooth; pour into cooled pie shell. Sprinkle with remaining crunch.

Meringue:
Combine egg whites and lime juice in a bowl. Beat until foamy with an electric mixer. Add sugar, one tablespoon at a time. Beat at high speed until stiff peaks form. Spoon onto filling. Bake in a preheated 375° oven for 10–15 minutes. Remove and let cool.

Gold Lattice:
Melt sugar in a heavy skillet over medium-high heat, stirring gently until syrup caramelizes and threads form off the edge of a spoon. The fewer times you stir, the easier it is to work with the syrup. Cool for 2–3 minutes in pan. Drizzle over pie creating spun look.

Grasshopper Pie

Easy

Serves 6-8
Prepare ahead
Preparation time:
*   30 minutes*
Chill 3 hours

5½ oz. chocolate wafer cookies, crumbled
2   oz. sugar
1½ oz. butter, melted
1½ tsp. gelatin
3   oz. water
2   oz. sugar
1   egg yolk
3   oz. creme de menthe
2   oz. white creme de cacao
2   cups whipped topping
Shaved chocolate

Crush wafers. Add sugar and butter and pat into 9" pie pan. Bake at 450° for 2-3 minutes. Soften gelatin in cold water. Dissolve over hot water. Beat in sugar and egg yolk. Add creme de menthe and creme de cacao. Chill until slightly thick. Whip topping and fold in. Put in shell and chill. Top with whipped cream and shaved chocolate.

Heath Bar® Ice Cream Pie

1¼ cups chocolate wafer crumbs
¼ cup butter or margarine, melted
12 Heath Bars®, refrigerated to harden
½ gallon vanilla ice cream, softened

Sauce:
¼ cup butter
1 cup confectioner's sugar
1 6 oz. pkg. chocolate chips
1 12 oz. can evaporated milk
1 tsp. vanilla

Easy

Serves 12
Prepare ahead
Preparation time:
 30 minutes
Freeze overnight

Freezes well

Prepare one day ahead

Mix chocolate wafer crumbs with butter. Line 9x12 pan with crumb mixture. Pat down and refrigerate until firm. Crush Heath Bars® by placing unwrapped candy in plastic bag and hitting with rolling pin. Mix with softened ice cream. Put in crust and freeze overnight. Serve with warmed sauce.

Sauce:
Melt butter with chocolate chips in top of double boiler and add confectioner's sugar and evaporated milk. Cook 8 minutes or until thickened. Add vanilla. Serve warm over pie.

Kahlua Pecan Pie

Easy

Serves 8–10
Prepare ahead
Preparation time:
 10 minutes
Bake 50 minutes

A new twist on an old
favorite.

Pastry crust (can be frozen pastry shell)
$1/_4$ cup butter
$3/_4$ cup sugar
1   tsp. vanilla
2   Tbsp. flour
3   eggs
$1/_2$ cup plus 1 tsp. Kahlua
$1/_2$ cup dark corn syrup
$3/_4$ cup evaporated milk
1   cup whole or chopped pecans
$1/_2$ cup heavy cream, whipped
Pecan halves

Line a 9" pie plate with your favorite pastry crust. Chill. Preheat oven to 400°. Cream together butter, sugar, vanilla, and flour. Beat in eggs, one at a time. Stir in Kahlua, corn syrup, evaporated milk, and pecans and mix well; pour into pie shell. Bake at 400° for 10 minutes, then reduce heat to 325° and bake about 40 minutes or until firm. Chill. When ready to serve, garnish with whipped cream and pecan halves.

Mocha-Fudge Pie

1   cup sugar
$^{1}/_{2}$ cup butter
2   egg yolks
2   oz. semi-sweet chocolate
$^{1}/_{2}$ cup sifted all-purpose flour
1   tsp. vanilla
2   egg whites
$^{1}/_{8}$ tsp. salt

Topping:
Coffee or vanilla ice cream, or whipped cream to which instant coffee crystals have been added. Leave cream rather soft.

Sift sugar. Beat butter until soft; add sugar gradually. Blend until creamy. Beat in egg yolks. Melt chocolate in double boiler; cool slightly. (When melting chocolate, do not overheat or it will congeal. If this happens, add $^{1}/_{2}$ teaspoon butter and stir vigorously.) Beat chocolate into butter-egg mixture. Add vanilla. Whip egg whites and salt until stiff; fold into batter. Pour into greased $8^{1}/_{2}$" pie plate and bake at 325° for no more than $^{1}/_{2}$ hour (should be soft in middle and crisp at edges). Serve cream or ice cream on the side. Serve cream in a silver sauceboat with ladle, or ice cream in balls, refrozen in a silver bowl and taken out just before serving so that container is frosted.

Easy

Serves 8–10
May prepare ahead
Preparation time:
 20 minutes
Bake 30 minutes

Freezes well

This is a devastatingly rich, crustless pie. Decorate with whole hulled strawberries standing on end, or candied violets and fresh flowers.

Open Sesame Pie

Moderate

Serves 8
May prepare ahead
Preparation time:
1¹/₂ hours
Chill 2–3 hours

A very early
Pillsbury bake-off
prize recipe.

Sesame pie shell:
3   Tbsp. sesame seeds
1   cup sifted all-purpose flour
¹/₂   tsp. salt
¹/₃   cup Crisco®
3¹/₂ Tbsp. cold water

Filling:
1   envelope unflavored gelatin
¹/₄   cup cold water
1   cup milk
2   egg yolks
¹/₄   cup sugar
¹/₄   tsp. salt
³/₄   cup heavy cream, whipped
1   tsp. vanilla
1   cup pitted dates, cut very fine
2   egg whites
2   Tbsp. sugar
Nutmeg

Sesame pie shell:
Toast sesame seeds in pie pan at 325° for 8–10 minutes until light golden brown. Remove seeds. Sift together flour and salt; add sesame seeds. Cut in shortening until particles are size of small peas. Gradually sprinkle water over mixture, tossing and stirring lightly with fork. Form into ball; roll out. Fit loosely into 9" pie pan; flute edges and prick with fork. Bake at 450° 10–12 minutes, until golden brown.

Filling:

Soften gelatin in cold water. Beat together milk, egg yolks, sugar, and salt in the top of a double boiler. Cook over hot water, stirring, until mixture coats metal spoon. Add softened gelatin; stir until dissolved. Chill until almost set, stirring occasionally. Fold in whipped cream, vanilla, and dates. Beat egg whites until slight mound forms. Add sugar gradually, beating after each addition until stiff. Fold meringue into date mixture. Heap into cooled pie shell; chill until firm. Sprinkle with nutmeg before serving.

Ponchartrain Pie

1	stick butter or margarine, melted
2	eggs, beaten
1	cup sugar
$\frac{1}{2}$	cup chopped dates
$\frac{1}{2}$	cup chopped nuts
$\frac{1}{2}$	cup shredded coconut

Unbaked 9" pie shell

Easy

Serves 8
Prepare ahead
Preparation time:
 10 minutes
Bake 38 minutes

This is an easy pie that gets raves.

Beat eggs, add sugar and beat. Add melted butter and mix. Add dates, nuts, and coconut and pour into unbaked pie shell. Bake for 8 minutes at 400° and 30 minutes at 350°.

Pumpkin Flan

Moderate

*Prepare ahead
Preparation time:
 20 minutes
Bake 1¹/₂ hours
Chill overnight*

*Serve with whipped
cream for a special
treat.*

Flan:

3	cups half and half
2	cups canned pumpkin (1 pound)
²/₃	cup sugar
¹/₄	cup rum
6	whole eggs plus 2 yolks, slightly beaten
2	tsp. pumpkin pie spice blend
1	tsp. salt

Topping:

¹/₂	cup sugar

Flan:
Combine all ingredients, mixing well. Pour into 9" non-metal dish. Set in pan of hot water. Bake at 350° for 1¹/₂ hours. Immediately on removing from oven, add topping.

Topping:
Melt ¹/₂ cup sugar in a small skillet until it is a caramel color. Pour over hot flan. Cover. Let set at room temperature for 2 hours. Refrigerate overnight.

Rhubarb Pie

2   eggs, well beaten with a spoon
    (do not use beater)
1   heaping cup sugar
3   heaping Tbsp. flour
2   cups rhubarb, cut up

Easy

Serves 6-8
Prepare ahead
Preparation time:
 10 minutes
Bake 30 minutes

Mix all ingredients together. Pour into pie shell. Bake 30 minutes at 350°.

Sour Cream Apple Pie

Easy

Serves 6-8
Prepare ahead
Preparation time:
 15 minutes
Bake 45 minutes

4–5 apples, peeled, cored and sliced
1   Tbsp. lemon juice
2   Tbsp. flour
³/₄ cup sugar
2   eggs, beaten
1   cup sour cream
¹/₂ tsp. vanilla extract
¹/₄ tsp. salt
1   9" unbaked pie shell

Topping:
¹/₃ cup sugar
¹/₃ cup chopped almonds
¹/₃ cup butter

Preheat oven to 350°. Toss apple slices with lemon juice and set aside. Mix flour and sugar together in a bowl; add eggs, sour cream, vanilla, and salt. Stir until smooth. Mix in apples and pour into pie shell. Bake at 350° for 30 minutes.

Topping:
Mix sugar and almonds together; cut in butter until mixture is coarse and crumbly. Spoon over pie and bake 15 minutes more, until golden brown. Serve warm or cold.

Restaurants

Arnold's

Garlic Butter:

3   cloves garlic, chopped
$\frac{1}{3}$ cup butter
$\frac{1}{3}$ cup olive oil
$\frac{1}{4}$ cup vegetable oil

Pasta:

3   oz. garlic butter
6   oz. raw seafood (cod, halibut, shrimp, scallops, and salmon)
$\frac{1}{4}$ sweet red pepper, cut in strips
$\frac{1}{2}$ small zucchini, sliced
3   water chestnuts, sliced
Hot, cooked linguine

Easy

Serves 1
Preparation time:
 30 minutes
Cook 10 minutes

Garlic Butter:
In skillet, sauté garlic in butter over low heat about 5 minutes. Remove from heat, add olive oil and vegetable oil. (Yields enough for 6-8 servings.)

Pasta:
In skillet, heat garlic butter and sauté seafood and vegetables, covered, over low heat about 6 minutes. Serve over linguine.

Blackened Lamb Chops with Jalapeno Mint Jelly

Crockett's

Moderate

Serves 6
Partially prepare
 ahead
Preparation time:
 15 minutes
Cook 4–6 minutes

This can also be
cooked on a grill over
an open flame.

Jelly:

1	1 lb. jar mint-flavored apple jelly
¹/₂	cup finely diced canned jalapeno peppers (reserve juice)

Lamb Chops:

4	Tbsp. paprika
2	Tbsp. cayenne pepper
1	Tbsp. onion powder
1	Tbsp. garlic powder
1	tsp. dry oregano
1	tsp. dry basil
1	tsp. dry thyme
12	1-inch thick lamb chops
¹/₂	lb. melted butter

Jelly:

In bowl, mix jelly and peppers together. Stir in some of the reserved juices for smoother consistency. Refrigerate.

Lamb chops:

Combine spices and mix well. Dredge the lamb chops in the butter, then coat well with seasonings. Place the chops in a white-hot 12-inch cast iron skillet; cook 2–3 minutes per side for medium rare. If blackening must be repeated, wipe skillet with a dry towel and let it get hot again. High temperature is absolutely necessary.

Orchids

2–4 lb. veal ribeye
16 oz. salmon fillet
12 oz. fresh spinach, blanched
6 oz. sole
3 oz. scallops
4 oz. heavy cream
Salt and pepper to taste
Dash cognac
1 tsp. paprika
1 tsp. cayenne
1 tsp. black pepper
1 tsp. thyme
1 tsp. garlic salt

Difficult

Serves 6
Preparation time:
 30 minutes
Bake 20 minutes

Butterfly the veal ribeye and pound to about one and a half inch thickness. Turn it over so outside is facing up. Split salmon fillet completely through the long side. Fillet should now be same size as pounded veal. Place salmon on top of veal. In food processor, mix together spinach, sole, scallops, heavy cream, salt, pepper and cognac. Consistency should be mousse-like. Spread over entire salmon area. Now begin at one end of roast and roll, tying with string to secure at end. Combine spices; mix well. Roll roast in spices and in heavy skillet, blacken entire outside of roast. Place in oven and bake at 350° for 20 minutes. Let rest 10 minutes and slice and serve.

Braised Golden Lamb Lambshanks

The Golden Lamb

Easy

Serves 4
Preparation time:
 15 minutes
Braise 1 hour

4   lambshanks (10–14 oz. each)
Salt and pepper to taste
4   Tbsp. butter or margarine
$1/_2$ cup whole baby carrots
$1/_2$ cup pearl onions
1   cup fresh mushrooms
$1/_2$ cup celery, cut in $1/_4$-inch slices
1   quart lamb stock, beef stock or bouillon
2   Tbsp. tomato paste
$1/_4$ tsp. pepper
$1/_4$ tsp. rosemary leaves, finely chopped
$1/_8$ tsp. thyme leaves
1   bay leaf
1   clove fresh garlic, minced
Chopped fresh parsley

Season lamb shanks with salt and pepper. Brown in butter in a Dutch oven. Add fresh vegetables and brown them also. Discard grease. Add stock, tomato paste, herbs and spices. Cover and braise in 350° oven until well done, about 1 hour. Skim off fat occasionally. Taste; add salt and pepper to taste. Sprinkle with fresh parsley and serve.

The Golden Lamb

$^1/_2$ cup sugar
1   tsp. dry mustard
1   tsp. salt
1   tsp. celery seed
$^1/_4$ tsp. grated onion
$^1/_3$ cup white vinegar
1   cup salad oil

Easy

Yield: 1$^1/_2$ cups
May prepare ahead
Preparation time:
 5 minutes

Mix all dry ingredients together. Add onion. Add small amount of oil; mix well. Gradually add small amounts of vinegar and oil alternately, ending with oil. Mix either in an electric mixer or blender.

La Normandie

Moderate

Serves 8–10
Prepare ahead
Preparation time:
 45 minutes
Marinate at least
 2 hours

Great for a summer
luncheon

Salad:
6   cups water
5   chicken-flavored bouillon cubes
1   tsp. salt
4–6 chicken breasts
$^1/_2$ lb. spaghetti (dry)
Garlic vinaigrette dressing (see recipe below)
$^1/_3$ cup mayonnaise
Soft lettuce leaves
$^1/_4$ lb. fresh mushrooms, sliced thickly
1   7 oz. jar marinated artichoke hearts
1   green pepper, cored, seeded and cut
     into thin strips
1   pint ripe cherry tomatoes, halved
1   cup thinly-sliced green onions or
     scallions

Garlic Vinaigrette Dressing:
$^2/_3$ cup vegetable oil
$^1/_3$ cup red wine vinegar
$1^1/_2$ tsp. minced garlic
1   tsp. salt
$^1/_4$ tsp. ground pepper
$^1/_8$ tsp. crushed red pepper flakes
1   tsp. dried basil

Put water, bouillon cubes, and salt in a large saucepot. Bring to a boil over high heat; add chicken, breast-side up, and return liquid to a boil. Reduce heat to moderately low; cover pan and simmer 25 minutes. Turn chicken, cover and simmer 20 minutes more. Meanwhile, cook spaghetti according to package directions; drain and toss with $3/_4$ cup of the dressing (reserve remainder). Cover spaghetti and refrigerate 2–24 hours. Remove and discard skin and bones from chicken; cut meat into 1 inch pieces. Add mayonnaise to meat and toss until well coated. Toss marinated spaghetti to separate strands; add chicken and toss again. Arrange lettuce leaves on a large serving platter or in a large salad bowl; top with spaghetti/chicken mixture and remaining ingredients. May be served immediately or covered and refrigerated for up to 4 hours. Remove from refrigerator 15–30 minutes before serving. Sprinkle remaining dressing over salad and toss.

Chester's Favorite
Leek and Potato Soup

Chester's Roadhouse

Easy

Serves 8
Preparation time:
 10 minutes
Cook 45 minutes

5   large baking potatoes, peeled and diced
1   whole leek
2   quarts chicken stock
1   small white onion
1   pint heavy cream or half & half
Salt and white pepper
2   green onions, sliced thin for garnish

Rinse potatoes and pat dry. Wash leek to remove any trace of grit, slice into thin one-inch strips. Place stock in a large heavy kettle. Bring to a boil, then add potatoes, leek and onion. Cook over medium heat for 10 minutes. Reduce heat to low and cook and additional 15 minutes or until potatoes are tender. Heat cream and slowly stir into hot soup mixture. Cook over low heat 5 minutes, whisking often. Season to taste with salt and pepper. Garnish with green onions and serve.

The Golden Lamb

2 green onions or leeks, chopped
1 onion, chopped
1 tsp. butter
$^1/_2$ cup celery, chopped
3 raw potatoes, peeled and diced
Dash thyme
4 cups chicken stock
Dash Tabasco
2 cups sour cream
1 cucumber, peeled and seeded,
   finely grated
Salt to taste
Chives, parsley, or dill for garnish

Easy

Serves 6–8
Prepare ahead
Preparation time:
  15 minutes
Cook 30 minutes
Chill several hours

Sauté onions in butter. Add celery, potatoes, thyme and stock and cook until potatoes are soft. Blend in a food processor until smooth. Add Tabasco, sour cream and cucumber. Mix well; add salt to taste. Chill several hours; serve cold. Garnish with chopped chives, parsley or fresh dill.

Chicken Paprikash

Grammer's

Moderate

Serves 5
Partially prepare
 ahead
Preparation time:
 15 minutes
Marinate 2–3 hours
Cook 50 minutes

Marinade:
5   boned chicken breasts
Pinch marjoram
Pinch sage
Pinch thyme
Dash white wine
1   tsp. oil
Paprika to cover chicken

Sauce:
8   oz. diced bacon
5   oz. diced onion
$\frac{1}{2}$ lb. quartered mushrooms
$\frac{1}{2}$ cup flour
2   Tbsp. paprika (sweet Hungarian)
$1\frac{1}{2}$ cups chicken stock
1   oz. white wine
Pinch thyme
Pinch marjoram
Pinch sage
2   cloves garlic, minced
1   bay leaf
Salt and pepper to taste

Marinade:
Place chicken flesh-side up on a tray, sprinkle
with a pinch of marjoram, sage, thyme and a
dash of white wine and oil. Cover with paprika
and marinate 2–3 hours.

Sauce:

In braising pan, render bacon until crisp, add onion and cook until clear. Add mushrooms, flour, and paprika. Cook, stirring continuously. When mixture is at a paste-like consistency, slowly add stock, wine, herbs, garlic and bay leaf. Let simmer until sauce is reduced to desired consistency. Salt and pepper to taste. Broil or sauté the chicken in butter for about 20 minutes, adding the sauce when served. Or, if preferred, place chicken in sauce after the stock has been added and simmer.

Garlic Shrimp and Oyster Pasta

Moderate

Serves 2
Preparation time:
 15 minutes
Cook 20 minutes

A favorite of chef
Jerry Hart.

The Heritage

2 quarts hot water
1 Tbsp. vegetable oil
1 Tbsp. salt
$\frac{1}{2}$ lb. fresh spaghetti or $\frac{1}{3}$ lb. dry spaghetti
$\frac{1}{4}$ tsp. black pepper
$\frac{3}{4}$ tsp. salt
$\frac{1}{2}$ tsp. white pepper
$\frac{1}{2}$ tsp. cayenne pepper
$\frac{1}{2}$ tsp. sweet paprika
$\frac{1}{2}$ tsp. dried thyme leaves
12 Tbsp. butter, divided
$\frac{1}{2}$ cup chopped green onions
8–10 peeled medium shrimp
1 Tbsp. garlic, minced
8 oysters, shucked and drained
$\frac{3}{4}$ cup warm dry white wine

In a large pot over high heat, combine hot water, oil and salt. Bring to a boil, add spaghetti and cook uncovered to al dente stage. Immediately drain the spaghetti into a colander and rinse with cold water to stop cooking. Combine black pepper, salt, white pepper, cayenne pepper, paprika and thyme in a small bowl. Set aside. Melt 6 Tbsp. of butter in a large skillet over high heat. Add the green onions, shrimp, garlic and spice mixture. Cook until shrimp turn pink (about 1 minute), shaking the pan back and forth. Add the oysters, wine and remaining 6 Tbsp. butter. Cook until butter melts and oysters curl (about 1 minute), continually shaking pan. Add the spaghetti. Toss to heat through, about 1 minute. Remove from heat and serve immediately.

Gouda Cheese
En Croute With Apples

Benson's Catering

1 4 oz. wheel of Gouda Cheese
1 egg, whipped thoroughly
1 5 x 5 inch pastry square
1 red Delicious or Granny Smith
   apple, sliced
2 sprigs parsley
6 oz. Thompson seedless grapes (optional)
Crackers (optional)

Easy

Serves 2-6
Preparation time:
15 minutes
Cooking time:
7-10 minutes

Brush puff pastry square with egg and wrap around Gouda cheese, making sure not to leave any part of the cheese exposed. Preheat oven to 375° for 15 minutes. Place cheese on a baking sheet and bake for 7–10 minutes. Brown the pastry under broiler for 15–20 seconds. Remove cheese from baking sheet and place on cutting board. Garnish with apple slices, parsley and grapes. Cut into 6 pieces and serve immediately. Serve crackers if desired.

Chester's Roadhouse

Easy

Serves 8–10
Prepare ahead
Preparation time:
20 minutes
Chill 2 hours

Freezes well

1 medium to large sweet onion, peeled and quartered
1 medium cucumber, peeled, seeded, cut in pieces
1 green pepper, seeded and cut in eighths
5–6 large tomatoes, peeled and cut in eighths
1 12-oz. can tomato juice
1 tsp. minced garlic
$1/_8$ tsp. ground black pepper
$1/_2$ tsp. chili powder
$1/_4$ tsp. tabasco
1 tsp. finely chopped cilantro
$1/_4$ cup light olive oil
$1/_4$ cup red wine vinegar
Croutons

In a food processor, chop first 4 ingredients separately to desired texture. Combine all vegetables and the remaining ingredients; mix well. Chill 2 hours. Before serving, top with croutons.

Grilled Duck Breast with Raspberry Barbecue Sauce

The Heritage

8	duck breasts, bone and skin removed
Salt and pepper	
1	cup onion, chopped
$^1/_2$	cup celery, chopped
$^1/_2$	cup green pepper, chopped
2	Tbsp. olive oil
2	garlic cloves, crushed
Pinch of cayenne pepper	
$^1/_4$	tsp. thyme
$^1/_4$	cup brown sugar
$^1/_4$	cup molasses
1	Tbsp. German-style mustard
1	bay leaf
$^1/_4$	cup red wine or raspberry vinegar
2	cups chicken stock
$^1/_8$	tsp. salt
2	cups raspberries, fresh or frozen

Moderate

Serves 8
Preparation time:
 15 minutes
Cook 45 minutes

Sauce can also be served with grilled pork or chicken.

Grill duck breasts over a hardwood fire, 2–3 minutes on each side for medium rare. Set aside. In a large saucepan, heat oil and sauté onion, celery and green pepper for 3 minutes. Add garlic, cayenne, thyme, brown sugar, molasses, mustard, bay leaf, vinegar, stock and salt. Stir to mix. Simmer over low heat for 20 minutes. Add raspberries and simmer 15 minutes. Purée sauce in food processor or blender in small batches. Strain. Serve sauce hot with grilled duck breasts.

Hungarian
Mushroom Soup

National Exemplar

Easy

Serves 4
May prepare ahead
Preparation time:
 10 minutes
Cook 40 minutes

4   Tbsp. butter
2   cups chopped onion
12 oz. fresh mushrooms, sliced
1–2 tsp. dill weed
2   cups stock or water
1   Tbsp. Hungarian paprika
3   Tbsp. flour
1   cup milk
1   tsp. salt
$^1/_8$ tsp. pepper
$^1/_2$ cup sour cream
Extra dill (optional)

Melt 2 Tbsp. butter and sauté onions; salt lightly. A few minutes later, add mushrooms, dill weed, $^1/_2$ cup stock or water, and paprika. Cover and simmer 15 minutes. Melt remaining butter in large saucepan. Whisk in flour and cook, whisking a few minutes. Add milk. Cook, stirring frequently, over low heat for 10 minutes, until thick. Stir in mushroom mixture and remaining stock. Cover and simmer 15 minutes. Just before serving add salt, pepper, lemon juice, sour cream and, if desired, extra dill.

Niçoise Salad

Benjamin's

4   handfuls romaine lettuce
24 cooked whole string beans
8   boiled new potatoes
16 pickled beets
28 cucumber slices, quartered
2   tomatoes, quartered
4   hard-cooked eggs, chopped
2   cups high-quality tuna
Sprinkle of chopped scallions
8   black olives (preferably Greek)
4   anchovies
4–5 Tbsp. vinaigrette

Easy

Serves 4
*Partially prepare
    ahead*
*Preparation time:
    40 minutes*

Clean romaine greens, dry with paper towels. Divide greens equally on 4 large salad plates. Add green beans on opposite sides of each plate, the same with boiled potatoes, beets and cucumbers. Garnish with tomato quarters and eggs. Cover middle of salad with tuna. Add onions and black olives. Curl an anchovy over the tuna. Pour dressing over all just before serving.

Raspberry Chicken

Maisonette

Moderate

Serves 6
Preparation time:
 20 minutes
Cook 25 minutes

Serve with rice or
potatoes

¼ cup oil
6   chicken breasts
1   cup raspberry vinegar
2   medium carrots, in chunks
2   stalks celery, in chunks
1   small onion, quartered
1½ quarts chicken stock
1   10 oz. can plum tomatoes, strained
2   cups heavy cream
3   Tbsp. Dijon mustard
1   Tbsp. fines herbes (equal parts parsley
     and green onion, chopped fine)
Salt and pepper to taste

Sauté chicken in oil until golden brown; remove. Deglaze drippings with raspberry vinegar; add carrots, celery, and onions. Add chicken to pan; pour in chicken stock, add tomatoes, bring to a boil. Remove from heat, place in a 350° oven. Cook for 20–25 minutes or until chicken is tender. Remove from pan. Blend sauce in food processor until smooth. Strain sauce. Place sauce back on stove; reduce by half. In separate bowl, mix heavy cream and fines herbes with mustard. Set aside until last minute. When sauce is reduced, pour in cream mixture, let boil a few minutes. Adjust seasonings with salt and pepper. Arrange chicken on platter and pour sauce over chicken.

Sauerkraut Balls

Grammer's

1   lb. dry mashed potatoes
1¹/₂ lb. sauerkraut, wrung out
4   oz. chopped ham
1   Tbsp. parsley
2   Tbsp. chopped scallions
1   Tbsp. mustard
Salt and pepper to taste
¹/₂   cup flour
1   egg
3   Tbsp. water or milk
1   cup fine bread crumbs

Combine first 7 ingredients and mix well. Roll into 1-inch balls. Dredge in flour. Beat egg slightly; stir in water or milk with a few gentle strokes. Dip balls in egg wash, then roll in bread crumbs. Deep fry or pan fry in oil until golden brown.

Easy

Serves 12–15
Partially prepare
  ahead
Preparation time:
  20 minutes
Cook 10 minutes

Shrimp Maisonette

Maisonette

Easy

Serves 4
Preparation time:
 10 minutes
Cook 5 minutes

1   Tbsp. chopped parsley
$^{1}/_{4}$ cup chopped shallots
1   Tbsp. minced garlic
$^{1}/_{2}$ cup softened sweet butter
Salt and pepper to taste
2   cups dry white wine
$^{1}/_{2}$ cup fish stock or water
12   large shrimp, peeled and deveined
16   mushroom caps, sliced
Toast

Combine the parsley, shallots, garlic and butter. Mix well. Add salt and pepper to taste. Melt butter in a heavy skillet. Add the wine and stock and bring to a boil. Add shrimp and mushrooms; be sure liquid covers all. Cover tightly and cook approximately $1^{1}/_{2}$–2 minutes. Spoon out shrimp and mushrooms with a slotted spoon onto hot plates. Reduce the cooking liquid by half; taste to check seasoning. Pour on shrimp and mushrooms. Serve with toast.